DRAWING
power

DEREK PRIME

SCRIPTURE UNION
130 CITY ROAD, LONDON EC1V 2NJ

© Derek Prime 1991

First published 1991 by Scripture Union
130 City Road, London EC1V 2NJ

British Library Cataloguing in Publication Data
Prime, Derek
Drawing Power
1. Bible. N.T. Acts. Critical studies
I. Title   II. Series
226.606

ISBN 0 86201 677 0

Scripture quotations in this publication are from the Holy Bible,
New International Version. Copyright © 1973, 1978, 1984
International Bible Society. Published by Hodder & Stoughton.

Phototypeset by Input Typesetting Ltd, London SW19 8DR
Printed and bound by Cox and Wyman Ltd, Reading.

CONTENTS

INTRODUCTION

When I bought my word-processor it wasn't long before I wondered if I had done the right thing. It all seemed so complicated! I began to think that I proved the truth of the old adage that it is hard for an old dog to learn new tricks!

I consulted the manual, of course, which came with the software I was using. But I was still daunted. What finally helped me make sense of the instructions were the *examples* at the end of the book. As I worked through them I saw what the manual was really getting at and, gradually, everything fitted into place.

The Acts of the Apostles is not a manual on evangelism. Luke, its writer, doesn't set out to explain what evangelism is or the principles by which it is to be carried out. The New Testament letters do that. But Acts does give us an enormous variety of examples which show how evangelism is worked out in practice. As we look at the examples, we'll find that the principles of evangelism taught elsewhere in the New Testament fit into place.

The book itself is the second half of Luke's account of Jesus' work – begun by him in person (described in

Luke's Gospel) then continued by him through his Spirit in the (church described in Acts).

Luke challenges us to remember two things in particular:

• the basic simplicity of the gospel message. It is all about Jesus Christ and salvation – the salvation that Jesus' death and resurrection have secured. God's command to all men and women everywhere is to repent and believe the good news. While much more can be said, that is the essence of the message. No matter how sophisticated society appears its need of salvation remains the same.

• the relevance of the gospel to literally everyone. In Acts it is preached to both Jews and Gentiles, whether king, governor, prison officer, soldier or business executive. No one is beyond the scope of God's saving purposes.

I hope that finding out about evangelism from Acts will fire you – as it has me – with fresh enthusiasm for sharing the good news about Jesus, the Son of God, the only Saviour. That is clearly one of the reasons why God the Holy Spirit has given us the book.

1

THE MESSAGE
IN
OUTLINE

Staying recently in a small hotel on the south coast, a couple at the same table as me were puzzled by a note they had found on their door. It simply said, 'Ring Ken.'

The problem was that they couldn't think of anyone called Ken who might possibly have rung them!

It turned out that the proprietor's son had been left on his own in the house. He had been told not to answer the phone while his parents were out but, when the phone rang, on impulse he answered it. Unfortunately, he didn't understand the message given to him to pass on, nor was he sure which guests it was intended for! So rather than do nothing, he stuck the note on my friends' door, hoping for the best. In the end all the guests were asking themselves if they knew a Ken, and whether or not they should ring him!

A new and startling message was suddenly brought to the people in Jerusalem when many were visiting the city for Pentecost:

'When the day of Pentecost came, they were all together in one place. Suddenly a sound like the blowing of a violent wind came from heaven and filled the whole house where they were sitting. They saw what seemed to be tongues of fire that separated and came to rest on each of them. All of them were filled with the Holy Spirit and began to speak in other tongues as the Spirit enabled them.

Now there were staying in Jerusalem God-fearing Jews from every nation under heaven. When they heard this sound, a crowd came together in bewilderment, because each one heard them speaking in his own language. Utterly amazed, they asked: "Are not all these men who are speaking Galileans? Then how is it that each of us hears them in his own native language? Parthians, Medes and Elamites; residents of Mesopotamia, Judea and Cappadocia, Pontus and Asia, Phrygia and Pamphylia, Egypt and the parts of Libya near Cyrene; visitors from Rome (both Jews and converts to Judaism); Cretans and Arabs – we hear them declaring the wonders of God in our own tongues!"

Amazed and perplexed, they asked one another, "What does this mean?'

Some, however, made fun of them and said, "They have had too much wine." '

Acts 2:1–13

Christians have been trusted with a message to pass on – the good news or 'gospel' of Jesus Christ. A messenger must know at least two things: the message he is to deliver and the identity of the people to whom he is to deliver it.

8

WHO IS THE MESSAGE FOR?

The message we have to deliver is intended for *all* people because it is the good news of how 'God so loved *the world* that He gave his one and only Son, that *whoever* believes in him shall not perish but have eternal life' (John 3:16). The message Peter first gave in Jerusalem on the Day of Pentecost was not just for the people of his day or for Jerusalem. It was for men and women of every age, and in every place.

WHAT IS THE MESSAGE?

Whether we make cement or a cake, we need to mix the ingredients in the right proportions! The same is true of the message of the gospel we are to share with others. We need to be sure we've got it right and that nothing is missing. Peter's message to the crowds on the Day of Pentecost had six essential ingredients. The better we grasp them, the better we will be able to communicate the good news to others.

1 The time has come!

The Old Testament – from the first promise of a Saviour in the Garden of Eden (Genesis 3:15) onwards – looked forward to Jesus' coming. The prophets were kept on tiptoe with excitement to see what God was going to do as he repeated his many promises of a Saviour (1 Peter 1:10–12). The promises spoke of a Christ who was to suffer and then come into great glory.

This promised One was to be the final Deliverer of God's people. He was called the Messiah or Christ (meaning 'anointed one') because he was specially chosen by God for a task no one else could do.

The Old Testament promises contained clues that God's plan of salvation was not just for the Jewish people, but for non-Jews as well. But the Jews found this difficult to take in – even Peter was quite horrified at the thought of receiving Gentiles into the church (Acts 10).

And it happened – all as prophesised in the Old Testament:

'Then Peter stood up with the Eleven, raised his voice and addressed the crowd: "Fellow-Jews and all of you who are in Jerusalem, let me explain this to you; listen carefully to what I say. These men are not drunk, as you suppose. It's only nine in the morning! No, this is what was spoken by the prophet Joel:
'In the last days, God says,
     I will pour out my Spirit on all people.
Your sons and your daughters will
          prophesy,
     your young men will see visions,
     your old men will dream dreams.
Even on my servants, both men and
          women,
     I will pour out my Spirit in those days,
     and they will prophesy.
I will show wonders in the heaven above
     and signs on the earth below,
     blood and fire and billows of smoke.
The sun will be turned to darkness
     and the moon to blood
     before the coming of the great and
          glorious day of the Lord.

> And everyone who calls on the name of the
> Lord will be saved.' " '
>
> *Acts 2:14–21*

Through Jesus, the 'Christ' or 'Messiah', God has made salvation possible for everyone who trusts Jesus for it. The prophets had also predicted that this amazing event would be confirmed by a great outpouring of God's Spirit, and this is what was happening in Jerusalem on the Day of Pentecost. It was appropriate that Peter should begin his sermon with the words, 'This is what was spoken by the prophet Joel . . .'!

What happened in first-century Palestine was not a surprise to those who genuinely looked for the promised Saviour. Men and women like Simeon and Anna knew God would keep his word (Luke 2:25–38).

When we share the gospel with others, it is important to explain that what happened when Jesus came two thousand years ago was a crucial part of God's eternal plan (see, for example, 1 Peter 1:18–21). This also underlines the Bible's reliability in what it promises. God's faithfulness to his promises in the past encourages us to trust his promises now, whether they relate to the present or the future.

2 God has visited us!

In Jesus, God has visited his world. Everything we could ever hope for – peace, wholeness, fulfilment, purpose – has arrived in him. In the coming of Jesus God has uniquely intervened in the history of mankind because Jesus is God's Son, God made flesh. The world can never be the same again.

It was clear that Jesus was the promised Messiah

because of the many miracles, wonders and signs he did – and there were many witnesses of these events. The four Gospels provide us with the details of Jesus' life. His miracles didn't simply show his power, but *who* he was. The Gospel writer, John, chose to relate just seven miracles that Jesus did, explaining them as 'signs', pointers to who Jesus was: 'These are written that you may believe that Jesus is the Christ, the Son of God, and that by believing you may have life in his name' (20:31). In talking with others about Jesus' life, then, we must talk about his miracles, and point out the evidence they give that he is God.

Significantly, though, each Gospel gives greater space to Jesus' death than to any other single event in Jesus' life. That was the most important thing he did for us, and we must always make this plain:

> ' "Men of Israel, listen to this: Jesus of Nazareth was a man accredited by God to you by miracles, wonders and signs, which God did among you through him, as you yourselves know. This man was handed over to you by God's set purpose and foreknowledge; and you, with the help of wicked men, put him to death by nailing him to the cross." '
>
> *Acts 2:22–23*

But the cross was not the end! The fact that Jesus was fully God, as well as fully human; the fact that he had committed no sins, so was perfect; and the fact that God had promised his resurrection, all made it certain that Jesus would rise from the dead. What's more, many people saw Jesus alive after his resurrection, just as many had witnessed his miracles. His resurrection was a *real* event in the real history of the world.

3 Salvation is now possible for all people

By his death and resurrection, Jesus overcame sin and broke its power over us. By doing this he has also opened the kingdom of heaven to all who believe in him. He has conquered sin in that it need no longer be an obstacle to fellowship with God. It can be justly forgiven by God because he has justly punished it – not by our eternal separation from God but by Jesus' death and separation from God on our behalf. We cannot be reunited with God by any other means: 'there is no other name under heaven given to men by which we must be saved' (Acts 4:12).

4 God really can save!

' "But God raised him from the dead, freeing him from the agony of death, because it was impossible for death to keep its hold on him.
David said about him:
'I saw the Lord always before me.
Because he is at my right hand,
I will not be shaken.
Therefore my heart is glad and my tongue rejoices;
my body also will live in hope,
because you will not abandon me to the grave,
nor will you let your Holy One see decay.
You have made known to me the paths of life;
you will fill me with joy in your presence.' " '

Acts 2:24–28

All human beings fear death; it is the great unknown. How can we be sure that Jesus' death means that our own deaths are not the end of us – or will not usher us into a worse, 'undead' existence? God has given us some proofs of the certainty of our salvation. The first is the resurrection of Jesus himself. The second is the powerful way in which Jesus, through the Holy Spirit, is working in the church today. And there is more: Christians today *know* the risen Jesus personally, and what God has done for Jesus he does for those who put their trust in him: showing us 'the paths of life', and 'filling us with joy in his presence'. Whenever we share the gospel it ought to be radiantly clear that we speak of a living Saviour!

The Holy Spirit, poured out on the church at Pentecost, is given to all Christians. He makes Jesus real to us, and convicts us of our sin and our need of God's salvation (John 16:8–11). Whenever we share the good news, therefore, we must depend upon the Holy Spirit's help. It is the Holy Spirit, ultimately, who will enable our hearers to make sense of the gospel.

5 This is only the beginning!

What God has begun, he will complete. Jesus will return to the world, this time as Judge, and God's kingdom will finally and unmistakably be established (see Acts 3:20–21; 17:30–31; 2 Thessalonians 1:7–10):

> ' "Brothers, I can tell you confidently that the patriarch David died and was buried, and his tomb is here to this day. But he was a prophet and knew that God had promised him on oath that he would place one of his descendants on his throne. Seeing

what was ahead, he spoke of the resurrection of the Christ, that he was not abandoned to the grave, nor did his body see decay. God has raised this Jesus to life, and we are all witnesses of the fact. Exalted to the right hand of God, he has received from the Father the promised Holy Spirit and has poured out what you now see and hear. For David did not ascend to heaven, and yet he said,

'The Lord said to my Lord,
   "Sit at my right hand
   until I make your enemies
   a footstool for your feet." '

Therefore let all Israel be assured of this: God has made this Jesus, whom you crucified, both Lord and Christ." '

Acts 2:29–36

Basic to the good news of the gospel is the hope that it brings – assurance about the future. Our Lord's purpose, which he *will* achieve, is to bring many sons and daughters to glory with him (Hebrews 2:10).

6 A response is needed

'When the people heard this, they were cut to the heart and said to Peter and the other apostles, "Brothers, what shall we do?"

Peter replied, "Repent and be baptised, every one of you, in the name of Jesus Christ so that your sins may be forgiven. And you will receive the gift of the Holy Spirit. The promise is for you and your children and for all who are far off – for all whom the Lord our God will call."

With many other words he warned them; and

he pleaded with them, "Save yourselves from this
corrupt generation." Those who accepted his
message were baptised, and about three thousand
were added to their number that day.'

Acts 2:37–41

When the facts of the gospel, and the evidence upon
which they are based, have been clearly stated and
explained, people must be challenged to act. What we
are told to do is to repent and be baptised in the name
of our Lord Jesus Christ. By doing this we publicly
affirm that he is our Saviour and Lord and receive the
gift of his Spirit, the Holy Spirit. We need both to warn
people of the consequences of rejecting Jesus and the
life he offers, and to plead with them not to ignore the
facts of their situation.

Peter's stress on baptism in evangelism seems a
little strange to our ears because differing views of baptism have, sadly, divided rather than united Christians.
As a result baptism is seldom if ever mentioned in the
context of united evangelistic campaigns. In Acts 2 it
was part and parcel of people's acceptance of the message about Jesus that Peter preached. In baptism they
professed their faith in Jesus as Lord, and their understanding that his death and resurrection were for them.
They declared his ownership of them. However, more
important than baptism is the faith it is meant to represent and express (a clear implication of Jesus' words
in Mark 16:16 and Paul's in 1 Corinthians 1:13–17).

Both repentance and faith must be carefully explained to those who are seeking after God. More than
being sorry for our sins, it means changing our mind
about sin itself and the wrong direction in which we

16

have been going. It demands a changed lifestyle because of a change of mind about sin.

Basic to telling people about repentance, therefore, is making sure they count the cost of becoming a Christian. John the Baptist spelt out the practical results of repentance whether for a civil-servant or a soldier (Luke 3:12–14). We must be practical and specific too, drawing honestly on our own experience. No one was allowed to become a disciple of Jesus without knowing first what was involved and how costly it might be.

Linked with repentance is faith. Faith is our response to God's character and promises. God has spoken to us through his word, the Bible, which proclaims the gospel to us. In this he calls us to put our trust in his Son, Jesus, the Saviour we need. The evidence of such faith is that we obey God – which is why the Bible speaks of 'the obedience that comes from faith' (Romans 1:5).

'Receiving' the Lord Jesus (John 1:12), 'coming' to him (Matthew 11:28–30), and 'calling upon' him for salvation (Romans 10:13) express in different ways the first steps of faith.

HOW MUCH DO PEOPLE KNOW ALREADY?

Our six-part outline is the framework of what we have to proclaim. In essence all the gospel is here. But it needs to be filled out, and applied in ways that fit people's circumstances and understanding.

It is important to remember that Peter was addressing Jews and converts to Judaism. He could take for granted that his hearers knew the Old Testament – so he could quote Joel and the Psalms without explaining why. He knew, too, that they took it for granted that the God who had given them the Old Testament Scriptures was also their Creator. Obviously, we cannot assume such understanding today.

We may need to explain why we believe the Bible is God's word. Rather than depending on our own words to explain the gospel, it is best to turn to the Bible itself, when possible. God's words, rather than ours, bring light, and our use of the Bible will often prompt people to ask questions like, 'Why do you keep referring to the Bible? How do you know it's reliable?'

Jesus' death on the Cross makes sense only when we see that it is God our Creator who has intervened to save us. John 1 is an amazing chapter to point people to: it declares that the Creator himself came into the world to save his creatures. The message of the Cross may not make sense to people because they do not understand that the Creator and the Saviour are one and the same.

Our chief task is to get people to see the meaning of Jesus' death. Paul summed up his message as 'Jesus Christ and him crucified' (see 1 Corinthians 2:2 and 1:23). But people will not understand why Jesus had to die unless, with the Spirit's help, we show them how much our sin offends our holy and good Creator.

What Jesus did on the Cross

A young man once came to see me, saying he wanted to become a Christian. I discovered he had been helped by the testimony of a group of keen young Christians. He told me that he had twice done what they said he should to become a Christian, but – to put it in his own words – 'it didn't work.'

They encouraged him to join in their witnessing. They assured him he had become a Christian because of the steps they had taken him through. But the more he tried to join them in witness, the more convinced he became that he wasn't really a Christian.

I suggested that the best thing to do was to try and start at the beginning again to see if there was anything he hadn't understood.

I fell into the trap of taking too much for granted, and of not starting back far enough. I began by talking about sin to see if he was genuinely convicted of his sin and his need of a Saviour. To my surprise there was no sense of sin at all. 'I don't really think I've done anything wrong,' he said.

We looked then at the ten commandments, and went through them one by one. I showed how we have all sinned by breaking God's Law. Conviction of sin began to dawn. Some of the issues the ten commandments raised prompted him to ask about the cost of following the Lord Jesus Christ. He was worried about the reaction of his friends and the changes that he would have to make in his life.

I got the impression that those who had first spoken to him had 'played down' the cost, perhaps afraid that they might put him off from becoming a Christian. So we considered the cost of discipleship as Jesus spells it out in the Gospels.

But then came the biggest surprise! I asked him about Jesus' death. 'Do you understand what Jesus did on the Cross?' 'No, I don't understand the Cross at all,' was his frank reply.

We arranged to meet again, and we read through Isaiah 53 and other passages. Soon God's truth began to fit into place and he saw what it meant to turn to God in repentance and to have faith in Jesus both as Saviour and Lord (Acts 20:21).

I didn't doubt for a minute the sincerity and enthusiasm of those who had first spoken to him. And there was no question, either, about the young man's desire to know the truth they had tried to share with him. But it wasn't enough to ask if he wanted 'to invite Jesus Christ into his life' without explaining what that meant. And it was certainly not right to say that he 'had become a Christian' simply because he said he agreed with what they told him.

It was when people were 'cut to the heart', that is, they fully understood their situation before God, and asked, 'What shall we do?' to put things right (Acts 2:37) that Peter was able to bring them to the moment of decision. By openly declaring God's truth, without compromise, Peter did his part (Acts 2:14–36), and God the Holy Spirit did the rest.

HEARING THE GOOD NEWS

Peter preached the good news of the Lord Jesus Christ on the Day of Pentecost. It was a message entrusted to him by God and confirmed to be from God by the dramatic events of that day.

Preaching is not limited to pulpits and platforms. After Stephen's death the early Christians were persecuted and Luke tells us that 'Those who had been scattered preached the word wherever they went' (Acts 8:4). The word translated 'preached' simply means 'shared the good news' – they 'gossiped' the gospel. But public preaching of the gospel – wherever it may be – is still God's chief means of bringing people to faith in Jesus.

Those who have the privilege of preaching the gospel from the pulpit depend on Christians to bring their non-Christian friends to hear. I was interested to discover how the members of the church fellowship to which I belong came to faith in the Lord Jesus. Forty-four per cent linked their conversion with being brought up in a Christian home – an encouragement and challenge to Christian parents. The second largest number – thirty-seven per cent – became Christians as a result of being invited to church.

Inviting people to church

It is important to bring people to hear gospel preaching because 'faith comes from hearing the message, and the message is heard through the word of Christ' (Romans 10:17).

We all have a unique circle of friends. My wife and I have a large number of acquaintances and friends in common but, because of the different things we do, my wife meets and knows people that I never do, and vice versa. If we added together our relatives, friends, fellow-employees, neighbours and acquaintances, the total number would probably surprise us. No relationship with anyone is 'accidental' because God chooses so often to work through contacts that seem at first to us to be casual and unimportant.

People who don't go to church are often much more ready to go than we imagine. They may just be waiting to be asked! That will certainly be the case if God's Spirit begins his unique work in their lives. We can be much too self-conscious or embarrassed about asking them. The best invitations we give are those which are natural and spontaneous but which, where possible, have been preceded by regular prayer for the people concerned. So how can we go about giving the invitation to come?

Here are just two ideas.
• On a Monday morning a colleague may ask you, 'What did you do over the weekend?' You could just say, 'Oh, I worked in the garden.' But suppose you heard a sermon on suffering. You could say, instead, 'Oh, I worked in the garden on Saturday and on Sunday I went to church and heard an excellent sermon on, "Why does God allow suffering?" '

'Oh, that's interesting,' may be the reply. 'So why *does* God allow suffering?'

In the course of your conversation it would probably then be easy to ask, 'Would you like to come along with me one Sunday? Why not come to church in the morning and join us for lunch afterwards? Or, if it suits you better, come to tea and go with us in the evening.'
• Your neighbours may sometimes share family problems with you. At the end of such a conversation you may often find yourself saying, 'I'll be thinking and praying for you.' Why not add something else that's part of your own experience: 'I find I get great help from God when I go to church. Would you like to come with me one Sunday? I'll be glad to call for you.'

Such opportunities are endless. The important thing is always to be prepared for them! Don't worry if a service to which your friend or acquaintance comes isn't evangelistic – that may even be an advantage! A service doesn't have to be directly evangelistic to lead to someone's conversion. When God's word is preached to believers, others listening may think 'Why doesn't this apply to me?' or 'Why can't I be as happy about these things as those Christians are?'

What if your friend, after talking with you, and perhaps coming with you to church, wants to find out more? Here are some ideas for how to help them:

• After a service, make it easy for your friend or neighbour to talk about what has been said if he or she wants to do so. If it comes naturally, you might like to open up the conversation, saying something like, 'I found what the preacher said challenging because . . .' If your friend doesn't then make the running, let the conversation move on to other subjects. God isn't in a hurry when he works in people's lives, and we should be patient, too, as we work with him.

• Have books or booklets at hand which explain the gospel, together with some which tell how others have come to find Jesus as their Saviour. But read them yourself first! You need to be able to recommend them honestly, knowing what's in them, and be able to discuss the contents.

• If your friend seems particularly interested, you could suggest meeting on a regular basis to study the Bible. It's ideal to work through a Gospel like Mark or John. Suggest a regular period of about thirty minutes each week. Limiting each session to half an hour means it can easily be fitted into most people's programme. It also allows time for the seed of God's word to germinate between sessions.

● If, during a conversation, you come up against a question you can't answer, don't be afraid to say so! But do offer to introduce the person to your minister or someone with more knowledge of the faith than yourself, so that your friend can get an answer. Alternatively, assure them that, though you don't know how to respond to their question now, you'll find out for them.

It is always helpful to have thought about the most likely questions that your friend or neighbour might ask. Part of loving our neighbour is making every effort to put ourselves in their position, so that we ask, 'What would I be thinking and feeling in their shoes if I were hearing me talk like this? What would I have asked if I was hearing the gospel for the first time?'

● While you are explaining the gospel, remember those six basic 'ingredients' we looked at from Peter's sermon so that people hear all the key facts.

● Have in mind a simple statement of the steps which people must take in order to receive Jesus as their Saviour and Lord. These would be, for instance: admit your sin; believe that Jesus died for you; receive him as your Saviour; publicly declare your faith in him. But before getting to that point, be sure that the person has *understood* the essential ingredients of the good news – *and* has a realistic idea of the cost. Otherwise he may end up like the young man I met who didn't really have a clue why the steps he took made no difference at all to him. It is important to explain, too, that the Holy Spirit is given to all who believe. He makes us sure of our new relationship to God and gives us strength to live for Jesus.

Finally, don't be discouraged if someone shows no interest in the good news. Don't be pushy either! Few people come to faith in Jesus through just one hearing of the gospel. God often uses many people – like links in a chain – to bring about a person's conversion. Encourage people to keep on coming to church, to listen carefully to the gospel as it is preached, and encourage them to keep asking questions and to say honestly what they think and feel about it.

God's co-workers

You will have many lovely surprises as you see God working in people's lives and as you see conversions which stand the test of time! Preaching away from home recently, I was delighted to see in the congregation a wife and husband with their teenage daughter. My mind went back twenty years. The phone had rung one evening, and it was the wife – then single. 'Mr Prime,' she said. 'Something has happened to me tonight – I think I've been converted!' The 'something' had happened while she was alone in her home as she thought about what she had heard. What had led up to it? She had come regularly to church, having been invited first to monthly guest services. But before coming to hear the public preaching of the gospel, her boss at work had witnessed to her. He gave her a Christian biography to read, and invited her to tea with his wife and himself and then to church. He and his wife did their part as did the preacher Sunday by Sunday – and God did his!

2

SEEING
THE
OPPORTUNITIES

One Sunday evening I preached on the Good Samaritan. As I shook hands at the door of the church, a woman said something rather quickly as she went out, indicating that God had spoken to her during the service. I didn't know her but a young woman was with her whom I later learned to be her daughter, and a Christian.

I discovered later that the mother had an acute physical problem which meant that she depended on various aids to get around. She couldn't even get in and out of bed without them. When she woke up the morning after I had seen her in church she felt she was being told by God to get up without resorting to the aids she always had to use. She did so, and walked unaided into her daughter's bedroom. When her daughter heard and saw what had happened, they both cried for joy at the mother's healing. The daughter then said, 'Mum, isn't it time you trusted in the Lord Jesus as your Saviour?' There and then she did so, as a direct result of her healing. Her conversion led ultimately to her husband's.

SIGNS AND WONDERS

The apostles' proclamation of Jesus was often linked with the dramatic healing of people – signs and wonders. Should we still expect signs and wonders to happen today? And especially when we evangelise?

'One day Peter and John were going up to the temple at the time of prayer – at three in the afternoon. Now a man crippled from birth was being carried to the temple gate called Beautiful, where he was put every day to beg from those going into the temple courts. When he saw Peter and John about to enter, he asked them for money. Peter looked straight at him, as did John. Then Peter said, "Look at us!" So the man gave them his attention, expecting to get something from them.

Then Peter said, "Silver or gold I do not have, but what I have I give you. In the name of Jesus Christ of Nazareth, walk." Taking him by the right hand, he helped him up, and instantly the man's feet and ankles became strong. He jumped to his feet and began to walk. Then he went with them into the temple courts, walking and jumping, and praising God. When all the people saw him walking and praising God, they recognised him as the same man who used to sit begging at the temple gate called Beautiful, and they were filled with wonder and amazement at what had happened to him.'

Acts 3:1–10

An example of 'power evangelism'

This miracle was only one of many. Writing the history of the early church was no easy task and Luke couldn't possibly have included everything that happened. He had to choose sample incidents typical of many others. In Acts 2:43 he says that 'many wonders and miraculous signs were done by the apostles.'

Are signs and wonders a necessary part of evangelism? One view is that they were given uniquely, or especially, in the first century – first to authenticate the ministry of Jesus and then to do the same for his apostles and their delegates. This view holds that we have no reason to expect similar signs and wonders after the New Testament period, and certainly not now.

Others, however, expect to see signs and wonders today and are inclined to view them as important and necessary evidence to the world that the gospel is from God. They believe that signs and wonders not only prepare the way for the full explanation of the good news but they also convince people of the gospel's truth and power. They are evidence of God's kingdom breaking into people's lives. This crippled man's healing certainly gave Peter and John the opportunity to tell him and the crowd the good news about Jesus.

As is often the case, truth exists in both extremes. There *was* something special about the apostolic period and the apostles' receiving of the Holy Spirit. Difficult as it may be, we have to try to distinguish between what was special to the apostles and what God planned to be normal for Christians thereafter.

Miracles – signs and wonders – had particular purposes in Jesus' ministry:
• They identified him as the promised Messiah. When John's disciples asked Jesus, 'Are you the one who was to come, or should we expect someone else?' Jesus replied, 'Go back and report to John what you hear

and see: The blind receive sight, the lame walk, those who have leprosy are cured, the deaf hear, the dead are raised, and the good news is preached to the poor' (Matthew 11:2–6). Jesus showed that the signs and wonders he performed were proofs of his identity for those who wanted to know who he was.

● They confirmed the truth of what he said. When Jesus declared that the sins of a paralysed man had been forgiven, the religious leaders of the day were scandalised. 'Who is this fellow who speaks blasphemy?' they asked. 'Who can forgive sins but God alone?' At this, Jesus went on to heal the man, so proving the truth of what he had said (Luke 5:17–26).

But the danger always was that people became more interested in the signs and wonders than in what Jesus had to say to them. He sent the crowds away when they became preoccupied with miracles, but seldom if ever when they genuinely wanted to listen to his teaching. Sometimes the signs and wonders got in the way because of people's unhelpful concentration upon them (see, for example, John 6 and the feeding of the five thousand).

As the signs and wonders pointed to Jesus' identity and the truth of what he said, so too the signs and wonders described in Acts confirmed the early church's testimony to Jesus' resurrection and the authority of the good news they proclaimed about him.

But it may be that the confirmation which signs and wonders gave was for a brief period only, and not God's permanent pattern. There is more than a hint of that possibility in what the writer to the Hebrews says about the message of salvation passed on to his readers by the apostles and their immediate successors. Having asked the question, 'How shall we escape if we ignore such a great salvation?' he writes, 'This salvation, which was first announced by the Lord, was confirmed to us by those who heard him. God also testified to it by signs, wonders and various miracles, and gifts of the Holy Spirit distributed according to his will' (Hebrews 2:3–4).

The first confirmation of the message after the resurrection was by the testimony of the apostles – by what they said, and by the transformation of their lives. They proclaimed what the Lord announced in his teaching. In addition, however, God added his own verification by 'signs, wonders and various miracles, and gifts of the Holy Spirit.' There are two hints that the latter are not the intended norm. First, the past tense is used – 'testified'. Second, it is stressed that God took the initiative, and that the gifts of the Spirit are 'distributed according to his will.' The Spirit alone determines what marks of power should accompany the preaching of the good news.

Sometimes he chooses to give signs and wonders, and sometimes he doesn't, as church history shows. He always acts in the interests of the spread of the gospel and the growth of the church. And he knows what will best glorify Jesus at any time. We should always be open to his doing the unexpected.

Do you believe in 'power evangelism'?

That question may well be asked. Not wanting to hedge or to avoid answering, I would have to ask first, 'What do you mean?' If someone is asking, 'Do you believe that miracles of healing like that described here in Acts

3:1–10 are necessary for effective evangelism?' then my honest answer is 'no'. It is 'no' because nowhere in the New Testament are we told that we should always link evangelism with signs and wonders.

Not all who witnessed the signs and wonders of Jesus' ministry, or those of the apostles, came to faith. The foremost example in the gospels is our Lord's feeding of the five thousand. When he followed this miracle with teaching about his Cross, most turned back and lost interest in following him (John 6:66). Similarly when Peter and John healed the crippled man at the temple gates, 'many who heard the message believed' (Act 4:4) but plainly not all.

Signs and wonders in the New Testament period were different from many which people claim take place today. All New Testament healings – whether by our Lord himself or his apostles – were complete and instant. People were healed at once, and it was obvious what had happened. That is certainly not the characteristic of much that is claimed today as signs and wonders.

That is not to suggest for a moment that God does not choose or may not choose to act in this way. But it points to the need for caution, and for wise testing of claims that are made. Satan himself can act supernaturally, and it is right, therefore, to test everything so that we avoid his counterfeiting of the good (2 Thessalonians 2:9). All who genuinely serve God will be glad to submit any claims they make to such testing.

I would not wish to rule out the possibility of miracles of healing, and I would not discount such as the means of a person's conversion, as in the case I have described. But that instance has not been the norm, and I do not believe that it is intended to be so. I, and, of course, others, have seen many conversions take place – including that of handicapped people – without such a sign or a wonder, and the conversions have been equally real evidences of God's power.

Evangelism with such signs is not superior to evangelism without them. I believe in 'power evangelism' in the sense that evangelism can be engaged in successfully only as we are filled with the Holy Spirit's power since the Lord Jesus said to the apostles, 'You will receive power when the Holy Spirit comes on you; and you will be my witnesses . . .' (Acts 1:8).

Paul's message and preaching 'were not with wise and persuasive words, but with a demonstration of the Spirit's power' (1 Corinthians 2:4). Some might argue that the 'demonstration of the Spirit's power' was by means of 'signs and wonders.' But Paul does not say so, and the record of his preaching in Corinth (Acts 18: 1–17) makes a number of statements about his straightforward preaching without any reference whatsoever to signs and wonders. The 'demonstration of the Spirit's power' describes the manner in which the word came home to them with 'deep conviction' so that the Corinthians accepted the message not as the message of a man but the message of God (see also 1 Thessalonians 1:5; 2:13; John 16:8–11).

One more thing must be said about 'power evangelism': to say or to imply that proclaiming the gospel of our Lord Jesus Christ *demands* 'signs and wonders' may well be a subtle denial of the unique power of the Cross. Paul's determination in evangelism was to know nothing 'except Jesus Christ and him crucified' (1 Corinthians 2:2). He actually played down the value of signs when he wrote, 'God was pleased through the foolishness of what was preached to save those who believe. Jews demand miraculous signs and Greeks look for wisdom, but we preach Christ crucified: a stumbling-block to Jews and foolishness to Gentiles, but to those whom God has called, both Jews and Greeks, Christ the power of God and the wisdom of God' (1 Corinthians 1:21–24).

It would be foolish and unrealistic to consider the work of evangelism from the Acts of the Apostles without relating ourselves to this subject, and that is why we have done so. The purpose in raising the issue is not to be controversial. We must respect the views of other Christians who think differently from ourselves. At all costs, however, we must maintain the purity of the gospel, and the centrality of our Lord Jesus and his saving work. We must not allow *any* emphasis to detract from the saving power of his Cross, and we must recognise that its message is foolishness to men and women until God the Holy Spirit shines into their hearts.

SEIZING THE OPPORTUNITY

There is something else crucial to notice about the incident at the temple gates: Peter and John seized on a God-given opportunity to witness to Jesus.

We often ask, with despair, 'How am I going to share my faith with others?' The answer sometimes is that we should not worry about it, but just let it happen!

The problem is that so often the people who talk and preach to us about evangelism are those who have a *gift* for it. They may forget that we're not all like them! We feel intimidated by them, realising we're not as effective as they are, unhelpfully anxious about why we aren't doing 'better'.

It's reassuring to remember that 'we are God's workmanship, created in Christ Jesus to do good works, which God prepared in advance for us to do' (Ephesians 2:10), and those good works include God-planned opportunities for us to share the good news of his Son. They will be varied and often unexpected. Our responsibility is to live the Christian life as we ought, and to be ready for whatever comes our way.

Unexpected!

This opportunity was unexpected and unanticipated. 'One day Peter and John were going up to the temple at the time of prayer – at three in the afternoon.' However many times before they had passed through the temple gate called Beautiful, *this* time was special. Since it was the daily practice to put the crippled man there, they must have seen him before, and heard his cries for money. But on this day it was different.

We may think of a new day as being just like any other, but a unique occasion may make it not the same at all. Potentially the opportunity may have been regularly present, but at the right moment it presents itself. That is how God works.

Taking the initiative

The man crippled from birth spoke first. 'When he saw Peter and John about to enter, he asked them for money.' The disabled man was, naturally, concerned about his material and physical needs.

But Peter took the initiative and turned to good

spiritual account this everyday occurrence of the man's plea for help. Peter told him, 'Look at us!' which was another way of saying, 'We have something better to give you.' Peter had Someone to offer him who is more valuable than all the gold and silver in the world!

If we have eyes to see and ears to hear, people will often say things which we may use to turn their focus away from the material and physical to the spiritual.

'What a frightening state the world is in – how is it all going to end?' What an excellent opportunity to speak of the return of our Lord Jesus! 'Yes, it is frightening. But I'm glad God *has* told us how it's all going to end.'

'Isn't it dreadful the way inflation increases and how one's money goes nowhere?' 'Yes, but isn't it good that the best things in life can't lose their value!' 'What do you have in mind?' 'I mean our health and important things like knowing God.'

'There's not much good news – if any – in the newspapers!' 'You're right there! There's really only one piece of good news that's for everyone – that's the good news of Jesus Christ.'

Such sample interchanges can sound artificial put down on paper. But spoken naturally and spontaneously, they may be openings for the gospel.

Dropping other things

Peter and John stopped. They were intending to go to the temple for the regular time of prayer – but they abandoned their plans in order to respond to this man's plea. They avoided the snare of the priest and the Levite in the story of the Good Samaritan who seem to have allowed duty to be their excuse for neglecting an opportunity to help a fellow human being.

Looking back, I feel guilty for those times I have been so busy rushing to church meetings that I haven't had time to talk to my neighbours who have been ready to chat. Passing the time of day with them, besides building up friendship, so often provides scope for Christian witness. We can sometimes hide behind 'church' or 'family' duties so that we fail to seize God-given moments for fostering good relationships.

Peter's witness was based on his confidence in Jesus and the power and authority of his name. 'Silver and gold I do not have,' he said, 'but what I have I give you. In the name of Jesus Christ of Nazareth, walk.' Peter suited his actions to his words as he held out his hand to the crippled man. The man 'jumped to his feet' – literally, 'he leapt like a deer.' This was more than a miracle, it was also a *sign* since a Messianic prophecy foretold: 'Then will the lame leap like a deer' (Isaiah 35:6).

Our confidence must likewise be in the power and authority of Jesus and especially – as the New Testament emphasises – in his authority to forgive sins because of his sacrificial death on behalf of sinners. We must suit our actions to our words, too. Having explained what Jesus can do for those we talk to about him, we need to encourage them to trust in him and prove his faithfulness to his promises.

As so often happens, the seizing of one opportunity led to another. The healing of the crippled man paved the way for the preaching of the gospel to the crowd that gathered. Peter went straight to the point:

'While the beggar held on to Peter and John, all the people were astonished and came running to them in the place called Solomon's Colonnade. When Peter saw this, he said to them: "Men of Israel, why does this surprise you? Why do you stare at us as if by our own power or godliness we had made this man walk? The God of Abraham, Isaac and Jacob, the God of our fathers, has glorified his servant Jesus. You handed him over to be killed, and you disowned him before Pilate, though he had decided to let him go. You disowned the Holy and Righteous One and asked that a murderer be released to you. You killed the author of life, but God raised him from the dead. We are witnesses of this. By faith in the name of Jesus, this man whom you see and know was made strong. It is Jesus' name and the faith that comes through him that has given this complete healing to him, as you can all see." '

Acts 3:11–16

Seeing the people's astonishment, Peter took the initiative. His approach is helpful. First, he carefully turned the focus of attention away from John and himself. People may sometimes make rather flattering comments: 'I wish I had the faith you have,' or 'I admire your confidence in God, and the kind of life you live.' While they may be genuine in what they say – and while what they observe may even be true! – we must take no credit for it but quickly turn their attention away from ourselves.

Second, Peter turned the focus of attention to God and his Son, Jesus, and to the central truths of the gospel: he recounted the facts concerning Jesus' death, and God's dramatic raising of Jesus from the dead. He affirmed the personal witness both he and John gave to Jesus' resurrection. He stressed Jesus' authority, and the faith in Jesus that God requires of us.

Those four points are essential in any sharing of the gospel:

- the purpose of Jesus' death;
- the significance of his resurrection;
- the witness we bear to the risen Jesus and his authority;
- the call to faith in him.

Unsheathing the sword

Peter then underlined what he said by reference to the Old Testament Scriptures, explaining exactly what was required of his hearers if they were to respond to the message of salvation:

> ' "Now, brothers, I know that you acted in ignorance, as did your leaders. But this is how God fulfilled what he had foretold through all the prophets, saying that his Christ would suffer. Repent, then, and turn to God, so that your sins may be wiped out, that times of refreshing may come from the Lord, and that he may send the Christ, who has been appointed for you – even Jesus. He must remain in heaven until the time comes for God to restore everything, as he promised long ago through his holy prophets. For Moses said, 'The Lord your God will raise up for you a prophet like me from among your own people; you must listen to everything he tells you. Anyone who does not listen to him will be completely cut off from among his people.'
> Indeed, all the prophets from Samuel on, as

many as have spoken, have foretold these days. And you are heirs of the prophets and of the covenant God made with your fathers. He said to Abraham, 'Through your offspring all peoples on earth will be blessed.' When God raised up his servant, he sent him first to you to bless you by turning each of you from your wicked ways." '

Acts 3:17–26

Although bold, Peter was courteous and sympathetic in his approach, as he showed his understanding of the ignorance behind their tragic rejection of Jesus. But knowing they understood the authority and inspiration of the Old Testament, Peter backed up what he said by quoting passages which confirmed the message.

The Scriptures are the Spirit's sword (Ephesians 6:17; Hebrews 4:12–13), piercing in their accurate pinpointing of our sin and need. As Peter wielded this weapon, just as he had done on the Day of Pentecost, the Holy Spirit brought understanding and conviction of sin, leading to the birth of people's faith in Jesus.

When we share the gospel, it is vital that we quickly get to the point where we open the Bible or the New Testament with people. It is essential that they know that we are not giving our own views or opinions but are sharing what God has said. His word has unique power and it is the instrument his Spirit delights to use.

Peter spelt out carefully the response God required if the people were to have their sins wiped out:

• They were to repent of their sins against God and the One he had sent – even though they had committed them in ignorance.

• They were to repent of their unbelief in Jesus up until this point in their lives.

● They were to turn to God by believing in Jesus, his Son, who suffered and rose again as the Old Testament Scriptures about the Messiah promised.

Peter assured them that they would then receive God's forgiveness, the first and loveliest benefit of the gospel. He expressed forgiveness in the picture of God wiping out their sins – rather like pressing the cancel button on a calculator to remove something from its memory.

No stereotype

Peter gave a full explanation of the gospel, although we only have a summary here, and it is similar to that which he gave on the Day of Pentecost. Yet it is not exactly the same because the hearers' starting point and circumstances were not identical. On the Day of Pentecost Peter had started with the Scriptures; here he concludes with them. The basic ingredients we identified in our last chapter are all here, but the wording and application are slightly different.

Sometimes Christians are encouraged to learn by heart a method of personal evangelism and then to apply this approach willy-nilly, even down to the exact words they use, to everyone to whom they witness. While God may sometimes graciously use such an approach, it is an unwise practice. It can lead to an unintelligent approach to evangelism and a lack of respect for a person's needs and questions. We can also find ourselves trusting in a method rather than in God the Holy Spirit.

On the Day of Pentecost Peter's starting point was his reply to the accusation that the disciples were drunk.

He explained, from the Old Testament, what was happening and then went on to the heart of the matter. In this instance in chapter 3 his starting point was people's surprise at the cripple's healing and their assumption that the power to heal was John's and Peter's own power. Peter went straight to the point, saying that it was nothing of the sort, rather it was proof of Jesus Christ's powerful authority. Having established this, he showed that salvation is even more important than healing.

To have in our mind various ways of presenting the gospel is obviously helpful, but stereotypes are to be avoided.

OPPORTUNITIES TODAY

What happened to Peter and John may not happen to us and, so far as we know, the same situation did not occur for them again. Opportunities vary in number and regularity. The best are those which arise unexpectedly and without any contrivance.

My wife and I were out for lunch with people we know well but whom we seldom see. The husband makes no Christian profession, and probably regards himself as anti anything religious or Christian, though not in a militant or hostile manner. The wife, on the other hand, goes to church. I admit that I didn't expect any opportunity for sharing or explaining the gospel. As I talked with the wife, she expressed her interest in alternative medicine and asked me what I thought about faith healing. Imagine my surprise, while I gave my answer, to hear the husband say to my wife, 'What's all this talk about "born again" Christians? What's meant by it?' Looking back, because we *were* so taken by surprise – to our shame – I don't think we seized the opportunities to the full. Even so, it led on to our sending them a Christian book, dealing with Christian basics, which it would not have been easy or opportune to send otherwise.

I'm in the middle of reading a book on the theology of the reformers – Martin Luther, Huldrych Zwingli, John Calvin and Menno Simons. I began reading it at the weekend on a train from Newcastle to Edinburgh. The young woman next to me looked over my shoulder and said that she'd just been reading an article in the newspaper which suggested that some books were bought and read for show. She asked if that was why I was reading such a solid-looking book! I explained I had been asked to write a review of it. 'For what magazine?' she asked, and I said it was for a Christian periodical. 'I've heard about Luther and Calvin,' she said. 'But who were Zwingli and the other man?' With all the initiative on her part, the opportunity to talk was there.

If we make a habit of reading a Christian book, perhaps on the way to work or in our lunch-hour, or leaving it on the coffee table when we have guests or visitors, there will be times when people ask, 'What are you reading?' Besides telling them, we may then offer to lend it to them once we've finished it.

Travelling, particularly on trains and planes, provides many opportunities for sharing faith. I find that when I ask God beforehand to help me to be prepared for them, and equip myself with suitable literature, the opportunities frequently arise. Or maybe it's just that I see them more readily than I would otherwise.

When your travel arrangements go wrong, rather than getting frustrated remember that God can turn it to a good purpose. Travelling down to London from Edinburgh by plane with a friend from Scotland, I arrived early at the check-in desk so that we could get seats together. But all to no avail! The flight was delayed because of a 'technical fault', and we were finally transferred to a smaller plane, where our original seat numbers were of no use. We got on almost last and had to find seats where we could. My friend sat in the row in front of me. Because of the flight delay conversation between passengers flowed as it might not otherwise have done. But I soon sensed that it had gone beyond the topic of flight delays, and the problem they cause, in the case of my friend. As he'd got talking to the man sitting next to him, he had a hunch that he was an alcoholic. At an appropriate point – when drinks were served by the cabin crew – my friend mentioned, as he declined an alcoholic drink, that he had once been an alcoholic. Immediately his seat-companion showed interest, and asked how it had happened and how he'd come through it. My friend told the story of his conversion, and they exchanged their names and addresses.

Crises arise not only in our own lives, but in those of relatives, colleagues at work and neighbours. A hospital visit, a promise to pray, an expression of concern, a letter with a helpful booklet, may all provide a unique opportunity – like that moment when Peter and John went up to the temple.

Some opportunities have to be earned. We may sometimes find ourselves really concerned for a person's spiritual need, yet feel that any direct approach to him or her would be unhelpful. Often, we need to win someone's friendship before we have the right to speak to them as a trusted friend. I heard of one person who undertook to help someone build a Welsh dresser in the hope that he might develop a closer friendship with him and so open the way to share the Lord Jesus with him. That could be a deceitful approach! But it won't be if we're motivated out of genuine love and concern for that person and allow him or her to make the running. People will seldom open up to us and ask us the questions they have until they feel they can trust us. We must prove ourselves trustworthy by living out the faith we profess.

Missed or seized?

Opportunities may be missed because we don't see them. We may fail to recognise them because we're not sensitive to what people are trying to say or to what their words and actions imply. Sadly, we may miss them because we're too busy doing other things, caught up with our own affairs.

Opportunities are lost to the lazy, and are captured by the diligent. Paul was aware of this, and he urged the Colossian Christian, to pray for him in his own sharing of the gospel: 'Pray that I may proclaim it clearly, as I should. Be wise in the way you act towards outsiders; make the most of every opportunity' (Colossians 4:4–5). Time is short, but opportunities are shorter.

3

POWER AND EQUIPMENT FOR EVANGELISM

As soon as some letters fall through the letter-box I recognise the handwriting; no need to try to guess who they're from! Some paintings don't need the name of the artist to be written underneath because the style is so distinctive. It's the same with the Acts of the Apostles: the Holy Spirit's unique activity is always present and often immediately recognisable to the Christian reader.

The book might be better described as 'the Acts of the Holy Spirit.' Luke himself gives it no title. If we could have interviewed the apostles and early Christians they would have been quick to acknowledge that the secret of their success was the gift of the Holy Spirit, just as Jesus had promised (Acts 1:8).

Much of the Holy Spirit's work is hidden from the human eye. But he is always active. Those who are effective in evangelism are aware of just how much they depend upon him.

The world at large, however, doesn't understand our dependence upon the Holy Spirit. That is to be expected since Jesus said, 'The world cannot accept him, because it neither sees him nor knows him. But you know him, for he lives with you and will be in you' (John 14:17). The knowledge the early Christians had of the Holy Spirit living with them, and in them, explains how they turned the world upside down for the sake of their Master's kingdom.

GOD'S AGENT

The Holy Spirit is the Agent of God's new creation in Christ – the church. He energises and empowers all who work to bring others into it.

If we look behind the scenes in the life of God's people, we soon find him at work:

> 'In those days when the number of disciples was increasing, the Grecian Jews among them complained against those of the Aramaic-speaking community because their widows were being overlooked in the daily distribution of food. So the Twelve gathered all the disciples together and said, "It would not be right for us to neglect the ministry of the word of God in order to wait on tables. Brothers, choose seven men from among you who are known to be full of the Spirit and wisdom. We will turn this responsibility over to them and will give our attention to prayer and the ministry of the word."
>
> This proposal pleased the whole group. They chose Stephen, a man full of faith and of the Holy Spirit; also Philip, Procorus, Nicanor, Timon, Parmenas, and Nicolas from Antioch, a convert to Judaism. They presented these men to the apostles, who prayed and laid their hands on them.
>
> So the word of God spread. The number of disciples in Jerusalem increased rapidly, and a large number of priests became obedient to the faith.'
>
> *Acts 6:1–7*

Bringing new members into God's family

The Holy Spirit was behind the number of disciples increasing rapidly and the delightful news of many priests becoming obedient to the faith. As one by one they made the all-important confession, 'Jesus is Lord,' it was the Holy Spirit who enabled them to do so (1 Corinthians 12:3). He it was who brought about the miracle of new birth in their lives (John 3:5–6), making them 'new creations' in Christ (2 Corinthians 5:17). He entered their lives as the gift of their risen and ascended Saviour (Romans 8:9).

Giving us help to sort out spiritual priorities

It was the Holy Spirit who helped the apostles understand their priorities when they faced this crisis over the care of widows: Greek-speaking Jews felt that the Hebrew widows were receiving preferential treatment. It would seem that up until this point the apostles themselves had taken responsibility for the daily distribution of food.

Jesus had promised that his Spirit would guide and teach the apostles. No doubt they prayed together about this early practical problem, and it became clear that they should not allow anything to divert them from their priority tasks of prayer and the teaching of God's word.

Giving us a sense of caring and love

It was the Holy Spirit who gave the disciples a sense of responsibility for each other. Although this chapter reveals a problem about the fair distribution of food and financial relief, we must not lose sight of the down-to-earth concern for others it shows the early Christians had. Large sums of money from the sale of possessions and property were placed in the apostles' hands for the use of the church.

The Holy Spirit binds us together as Christians in spiritual unity, teaching us to love one another and to express that love in practical ways (Romans 15:30; Galatians 5:22; 6:10).

Giving us a unity that overcomes difficulties

It was the Holy Spirit who gave the members of the church grace to overcome the feeling of grievance that existed, and to show their unity in the Lord Jesus. The New Testament, like the Bible as a whole, is completely honest, and never covers up problems. It cannot have been easy for the apostles to accept criticism over their handling of the food distribution. But there is no hint that they tried to justify themselves. Rather, they immediately tried to put right what was wrong, in an 'effort to keep the unity of the Spirit through the bond of peace' (Ephesians 4:3), a priority to which the Holy Spirit always calls us.

Giving guidance about office-bearers

The Holy Spirit also guided the church in the choice of the seven. It is the Holy Spirit who raises up leaders in the church (Acts 20:28) and helps Christ's people to recognise the necessary spiritual qualities in those whom they call to office. All seven of these men had Greek names and seem to have been Greek-speaking members of the church, the group that complained of being overlooked. More important, however, than their national and language background was their reputation as men 'full of the Spirit and wisdom.'

The special interest of the appointment of the seven is that it introduces Stephen and Philip to us, although the spotlight in this chapter, and the one that follows, is upon Stephen. Both were powerful witnesses to the Lord Jesus, and Philip is later described as an evangelist (Acts 21:8).

Introduced to us as men who were full of the Spirit and of wisdom, we are reminded that it is who we are – our characters – that is of first importance in evangelism. How we live must match what we say. The truth of our testimony to the Lord must be proved by our character and behaviour. We cannot share the gospel with integrity unless our lives give a model for others to follow (see, for example, 1 Thessalonians 1:6–7). Stephen practised the gospel he preached. Gifts for evangelism are of little use without Christ-like character.

Giving us direction in prayer

In was the Holy Spirit who directed the apostles in their prayers, and confirmed the decision of the church. As they asked for his help he prompted them to pray for the right things, and put the words into their mouths. He works in the same way with us, giving us a compelling concern for those people and events he calls us to pray for. As the apostles laid their hands on the seven, they recognised them as God's choice and prayed for his will to be done through them. It would be interesting to know what they prayed. Did they pray, 'Lord guide your servants into all your will for them, whatever that may be'? Certainly for both Stephen and Philip one assignment in God's service quickly led to another they probably did not foresee at that earlier time of prayer.

Stephen became the first Christian martyr, and Philip the first Christian to be described in the New Testament as an evangelist.

Giving us his fulness

'Now Stephen, a man full of God's grace and power, did great wonders and miraculous signs among the people. Opposition arose, however, from members of the Synagogue of the Freedmen (as it was called) – Jews of Cyrene and Alexandria as well as the provinces of Cilicia and Asia. These men began to argue with Stephen, but they could not stand up against his wisdom or the Spirit by which he spoke.

Then they secretly persuaded some men to say, "We have heard Stephen speak words of blasphemy against Moses and against God."

So they stirred up the people and the elders and the teachers of the law. They seized Stephen and brought him before the Sanhedrin. They produced false witnesses, who testified, "This fellow never stops speaking against the holy place and against the law. For we have heard him say that this Jesus of Nazareth will destroy this place and change the customs Moses handed down to us."

All who were sitting in the Sanhedrin looked intently at Stephen, and they saw that his face was like the face of an angel.'

Acts 6:8–15

The first thing we know about Stephen on the spiritual level is that he was recognised to be full of the Spirit. This was shown by Stephen's thirsting after the Lord Jesus, and his delight in trusting and obeying him. That obedience led, in turn, to his sharing the good news of Jesus with others.

Today, people are telling us many different things

about what our attitude to the Holy Spirit should be, and about how we should expect to experience his work in our lives. In these things we should always be guided by what the Bible teaches. There is, for example, no specific *command* in the New Testament to be baptised with the Spirit, or to speak in tongues, but we *are* all instructed to be 'filled' with the Spirit (Ephesians 5:18).

To be filled with the Spirit is to be filled with God's power to do his will – whether in being the kind of people we ought to be or in the service he gives us to do. Just as we keep on going back to God for forgiveness every time we are aware of sin, so we must go back to him time and again to be refilled with his Spirit as often as we feel our need of his strength and power. When we have the privilege of talking to others about Jesus, we will especially feel our need of his empowering.

In the New Testament, mention of the Holy Spirit's power is often linked with obedience to Jesus' last commission to his disciples to preach the good news to everyone. Filled with the Spirit, Stephen found himself in the thick of evangelism. Let us now focus our attention upon him, and pick out the signs of the Holy Spirit's work in Stephen's life.

Giving spiritual gifts

The Holy Spirit equipped Stephen with spiritual gifts, and it is no accident that the Spirit is mentioned three times in this passage.

He distributes different gifts to Christians, just as varied functions are given to the various parts of our body (Romans 12:6–8). Christians are given their gifts by the Spirit that they may use them for the good of the rest of the body of Christ (1 Corinthians 12:4–11).

By this means he equips God's people for the building up of the church (Ephesians 4:11–13).

The first gift he gave to Stephen was obviously the gift of administration. His evangelistic ability does not seem to have been obvious at first. Some spiritual gifts do not appear straight away in our lives. Circumstances may give rise to their discovery later. Stephen was willing to do whatever tasks were given him – a mark of someone filled with the Spirit of Christ. A spiritual apprenticeship in humdrum and very ordinary tasks is often necessary before we can be entrusted with greater responsibilities. Faithfulness in one sphere leads to opportunities in another. For example, a young married man was asked to help the church secretary to arrange interviews for those applying for church membership. It was basically an administrative job, but it soon developed into something more. Every time someone was due for interview, he and his wife invited the prospective member to tea beforehand, then introduced them to the elders. Afterwards, he and his wife carefully kept in touch with the new members until they were well integrated into the life of the fellowship. It wasn't long before the church recognised that this man had the gifts of an elder.

Giving a desire to share the gospel

The Holy Spirit gave Stephen the desire and ability to share the gospel. In every period of history the Spirit raises up messengers and directs them to people at the right time (see Acts 13:2–4; 16:6–10). We cannot be dogmatic about Stephen's possessing the gift of an evangelist, although Philip, as we have said, is described as such (Acts 21:8). The term 'evangelist' is found only three times in the New Testament, and little is said about the gift. The evangelists of the New Testament may have been more like pioneer missionaries than contemporary evangelists. Nevertheless some Christians have a gift for getting alongside people and communicating the gospel with an ease others of us do not possess.

All of us, however, are called to witness, whether we *feel* specially gifted or not. That may be why Paul urged Timothy to 'do the work of an evangelist' (2 Timothy 4:5). Timothy may have felt he was not gifted in this way but that was no reason to shirk reaching out to those who didn't yet know Christ. A genuine Christian lifestyle and assurance for the future will provoke people to question us about our faith in Christ, so giving us opportunities to witness to them. Peter encourages us to 'always be prepared to give an answer to everyone who asks you to give the reason for the hope that you have. But,' he said, 'do this with gentleness and respect' (1 Peter 3:15–16).

Stephen did not confuse social action with evangelism. There is a place for both, but they are different things. Overwhelmed by the crying needs of society, we can easily feel it our responsibility to remedy specific social ills. It is certainly right to be concerned in this way – and to do what we can to put things right. But social concern must never *take the place* of straightforward evangelism. Social action is not evangelism, nor should it be thought of primarily as a means of evangelism; we are obliged to help people where they need help, simply because they need it. At the same time we need to remember that the urgent need of everyone

– whether socially or economically deprived or not – is to know Jesus Christ as their Saviour.

One purpose of the description of Stephen and his work, in chapter 6, is to give a lead into his important speech before the Sanhedrin, in chapter 7. In this speech he showed that Jesus was really the promised Messiah, and affirmed his personal faith in him as the One who fulfils all the hopes and promises of the Old Testament. In this, too, Stephen was doing the work of an evangelist. Chapter 6 provides many instances of the way in which the Holy Spirit equips us to witness.

Giving confidence in God

The Holy Spirit made Stephen confident in God – he was 'a man full of faith and of the Holy Spirit'. This is another way of saying that Stephen's faith was easily seen. The Holy Spirit encourages our faith in God as he increases our understanding of God's character, his world, and the greatness of his Son, our Saviour. We have to play our part in this by giving him time to speak to us – by reading the Scriptures and meditating on who Jesus is, what he has done and is still doing for us.

Giving graciousness

The Holy Spirit helped Stephen to be gracious – he was 'full of God's grace and power'. The apostles testified that the main characteristics of Jesus that stuck in their minds after their years with him were his grace and truth (John 1:14). As we try to win others to Jesus we have no option but to speak the truth about sin, judgment, and our personal responsibility for a right response to God. But we must speak the truth graciously. If we are filled with the Spirit, our attitude towards others will be marked by gentleness. We will speak the truth, but we will speak it lovingly, so that our hearers see we have no pleasure in confronting them with sin and its consequences, but only a real love for them and a genuine desire that they might know the eternal salvation Jesus Christ came to bring.

Giving power

The Holy Spirit made Stephen's testimony powerful, and confirmed his work by 'great wonders and miraculous signs'. Stephen was full not only of grace but of spiritual authority. The Holy Spirit delights to accompany faithful preaching of the gospel with the awareness of God's presence and with powerful results (1 Corinthians 2:1–5). The apostles and early Christians knew this to be the explanation of the authority which others recognised in what they said. 'Our gospel came to you not simply with words,' Paul wrote to the Thessalonians, 'but also with power, with the Holy Spirit and with deep conviction' (1 Thessalonians 1:5). What we said in the last chapter about 'great wonders and miraculous signs' applies to Stephen's ministry. He is the first Christian other than the apostles who is said to have had such signs characterise his ministry. It may be significant that he – together with the other six men – had the apostles' hands laid upon him, and the apostles may have prayed that the seven might know these signs accompanying their work.

Giving concern for people's salvation

The Holy Spirit gave Stephen a great concern for the salvation of his own people, that is, the 'Hellenistic' or Greek-speaking Jews – those from Cyrene and Alexandria as well as the provinces of Cilicia and Asia.

When Jesus looked at the crowds, 'he had compassion on them, because they were harassed and helpless, like sheep without a shepherd' (Matthew 9:36). When we are filled with his Spirit, we possess his mind, and feel and see as he does. Stephen felt what the apostle Paul later expressed to the Romans. 'I have great sorrow and unceasing anguish in my heart . . . My heart's desire and prayer to God for the Israelites is that they may be saved' (Romans 9:2; 10:1).

The Holy Spirit makes us feel responsibly concerned for people, beginning with those closest to us (Acts 1:8). We cannot be truly open to the Spirit without being willing to engage in evangelism. All the time there are people ignorant of God we have a duty to speak the good news to them (1 Corinthians 15:34). It is a sin to withhold it or to be blind to their desperate plight.

Our whole behaviour is to have the salvation of others in view. Our aim must not be to live as we please, but to live so that others may be attracted to our Saviour. It was out of Stephen's concern for his own people that the development of his evangelistic gift arose, and that is often the way. We see a need, and we feel that we must try to meet it. In so doing, we discover we have gifts – or perhaps the Holy Spirit gives new gifts – to achieve the task. More important than evangelistic gifts, therefore, is a spiritual concern for people's salvation. And that the Spirit always gives us if we are open to him.

Giving strength in the face of opposition

The Holy Spirit sustained Stephen as he faced severe hostility. Evangelism in the power of the Spirit always provokes opposition from Satan, who is concerned only to destroy and tear people apart. It is this which makes evangelism such hard work.

The opposition may be from our own family. An elder of a parish church attended an evangelistic meeting. He had never really understood the gospel until that night and, brought under conviction of sin, he put his trust in Jesus. I doubt if his minister appreciated being asked by him the following Sunday why this same gospel was not preached in his church! But the most severe antagonism to his conversion, and to what he now believed, came from his wife, and he had to endure it over a long period. Some while later she responded to his witness to her. But the opposition had been real.

The hostile reaction to Stephen's witness was the start of the persecution of the early Christians living in Jerusalem, and it came to a head in a great scattering of believers throughout Judea and Samaria (Acts 8:1).

False witnesses were used to discredit Stephen, as with our Lord. But that shouldn't take us by surprise. Jesus himself had warned, 'Remember the words I spoke to you: "No servant is greater than his master." If they persecuted me, they will persecute you also' (John 15:20).

Enabling right answers to be given

The Holy Spirit directed Stephen's answers when he was under such intense pressure, putting the thoughts and words into his mind. The members of the Synagogue of the Freedmen 'began to argue with Stephen, but they could not stand up against his wisdom or the Spirit by which he spoke'. Note the reference to the

Holy Spirit, and the wisdom given Stephen. He proved the truth of Jesus' promise: 'I will give you words and wisdom that none of your adversaries will be able to resist or contradict' (Luke 21:15). The Holy Spirit's power and wisdom are not given, though, before we need them; only *as* we require them. In other words, if we simply wait until we feel we have them before saying anything, we will probably say nothing! But when we are obedient to our Lord's command to evangelise, we will find that his power is present, and the answers are given us when we are challenged and questioned.

Always being present

The Holy Spirit was clearly present with Stephen. There is no need to draw any distinction between the presence of the Spirit and that of Jesus, since it is the Spirit who makes us aware of our Saviour's closeness. Stephen was radiant in a way that was somehow supernatural; Luke describes his face as being 'like the face of an angel'. This fits in with Peter's encouragement to Christians to witness, no matter how great the opposition they receive: 'If you are insulted because of the name of Christ, you are blessed, for the Spirit of glory and of God rests on you' (1 Peter 4:14). All who seize the opportunities of one-to-one witness, will testify that they are never more aware of the Lord's presence with them than when they open their mouths and speak a good word for him.

Giving skill in spiritual swordsmanship

The Holy Spirit gave Stephen skill in 'spiritual swordsmanship'. In his powerful speech before the Sanhedrin (chapter 7) Stephen gave a panoramic view of the whole of the Old Testament, skilfully showing how all its prophecies pointed to Jesus. In a masterly fashion he presented the case for belief in Jesus as the Christ against those who argued against him. In doing this he was wielding 'the sword of the Spirit', which is the word of God (Ephesians 6:17). Stephen knew the Scriptures and how to use them. The Scriptures helped him see that it was inevitable that the young church should break away from Judaism. The Holy Spirit prompted Stephen to remember, quote and apply the Scriptures to the situation in which he and his hearers found themselves.

The Bible is the Spirit's sword. Its unique authorship means it has unsurpassed power to get through where our words cannot. It is given to us to know and use. Filled with the Spirit, we can use the Spirit's sword confidently and prove its power. The enemy of our souls will, however, try to put us off using it. He'll make us think that people won't like us reading the Bible to them, or that they'll think we're old-fashioned if we do. He tries this on because he knows from experience the real force of the Bible (see Matthew 4:4–10).

As I have tried to get the message of the gospel across to someone in my own words, I've sometimes struggled, feeling more and more ineffective. I've then been prompted to remember my 'sword'. Producing my Bible or New Testament, I've said, 'Let me read Jesus' words . . .' or 'Let me share what the Bible says . . .' So often that has been the turning-point in the conversation: God's word has brought light where my words simply haven't.

Giving a vision of Christ

The Holy Spirit gave Stephen the strength to endure (Acts 7:55–56). If we are to carry on sharing our faith – whether in door-to-door visiting or witnessing to members of our families – we need 'stickability'. Opposition is itself off-putting, but we might also gradually become discouraged by lack of response.

At the end of chapter 7, Luke gives a significant clue to Stephen's power to endure: his hopes and attention were fixed on his all-sufficient Saviour. 'Stephen, full of the Holy Spirit, looked up to heaven and saw the glory of God, and Jesus standing at the right hand of God.' It was as he obeyed his Lord in testifying about him that Stephen experienced the Spirit's strength and power.

Everywhere else in the New Testament the ascended Jesus is pictured as *sitting* at God's right hand, a symbolic phrase to emphasise that his work is completed. Here he *stands*, as a sign of his readiness to help Stephen and, soon, to receive him into his presence. This vision of Jesus – a vision of faith – sustained him.

As we fix our eyes on Jesus we can't help but remember all he has done for us – especially by his Cross. Our burning motive for telling others about him then becomes gratitude. We see afresh what a privilege it is to serve him, and feel again the excitement of sharing in his final triumph.

Enabling Christlikeness

The Holy Spirit enabled Stephen to follow Jesus' example of love in praying for his enemies. Again, Stephen could do this only because he had glimpsed Jesus' glory. As we fix our eyes on Jesus we are transformed, more and more, into his likeness (2 Corinthians 3:18). Being Christlike doesn't always go down well, though! The crowd were furious at Stephen's witness and stoned him to death. As he died Stephen followed his Master's example of committing his spirit to God and praying for his enemies, 'Lord, do not hold this sin against them.'

The Holy Spirit always encourages and prompts us to love (Galatians 5:22; 2 Corinthians 5:14–15). The real test of love is how we view those who regard themselves as our enemies. To win others we must be ready to give ourselves to and for them in any way God wants (1 Thessalonians 1:5; 2:8). The implications of this are enormous and can be extremely costly. It is helpful to look back to remember the time, patience and love that others gave us when *we* were looking for God.

Giving conviction of sin and need

The Holy Spirit used Stephen's example to sow the seeds of conviction of sin in at least one person that day who saw himself as Stephen's enemy. Luke obtained much of his information from the apostle Paul, so it is telling that he notes that those who stoned Stephen 'laid their clothes at the feet of a young man named Saul. And Saul was there, giving approval to his death' (Acts 7:58; 8:1). Remembering that Paul came from Cilicia, it may also be significant that the Synagogue of the Freedmen from which the original opposition came was made up of 'Jews of Cyrene and Alexandria as well as the provinces of Cilicia and Asia' (Acts 6:9).

Paul heard Stephen's speech and saw his Christlikeness. There seems little doubt that the Holy Spirit used these things to sow the seeds of conviction in his heart.

61

Later on, giving his testimony before Agrippa, Paul described how the Lord had asked him, pointedly, 'Saul, Saul, why do you persecute me? It is hard for you to kick against the goads' (Acts 26:14). Perhaps the first of those 'goads' was Stephen's testimony.

It is the Holy Spirit's work to show men and women their need of salvation as he convicts them of their sin, and especially their sin in not believing in the Lord Jesus Christ (John 16:8–11). As we share the good news of Jesus, we may be sure that the Holy Spirit will do his accompanying work of conviction. We are workers together with God.

Giving new beginnings

Stephen's work was now over, but not that of others. His death was followed by the church's widespread persecution – its first taste of it. 'All except the apostles were scattered throughout Judea and Samaria' (Acts 8:1). But God was in control. 'Those who had been scattered preached the word wherever they went' (8:4). They were not evangelists, just as the great majority of us are not evangelists, simply faithful Christians prepared to share the good news. As for Philip, who was an evangelist, he 'went down to a city in Samaria and proclaimed the Christ there' (8:5).

The more the early Christians shared their faith the more skilful they became. That was certainly the case for Philip as he exercised his evangelistic gift. All gifts, like muscles, develop with use. The more we use them, the stronger they become. But whether we think of Stephen, these scattered and anonymous Christians or Philip, they were all equally dependent on the Holy Spirit to actually bring about conversions.

4

THE DIRECTOR
OF EVANGELISM

The actor, David Suchet, was interviewed on the radio. At the time he was playing the part of the dapper Belgian detective, Hercule Poirot, in a series of television adaptations of Agatha Christie stories. He happened to comment that on one occasion he had gone over to America as an agnostic and had come back a Christian – all because of a Bible he had read during his trip.

Gideons listening to the interview pricked up their ears, and their Executive Director wrote to Mr. Suchet asking if the Bible had been one placed by the Gideons. This is the courteous and encouraging reply the Director received:

'Many thanks indeed for your letter . . . It was indeed a "Gideon" Bible that set me on my way and has often *kept* me on the way since . . .

'A very brief account of what happened is this – while lying in the bath I felt a desperate need to read the Bible. Why? I don't know. (I hadn't read any of it since my schooldays!) It was late at night – no shops open or churches to go to. So, shrugging my shoulders, I went to bed and went to take my book out of the top drawer of the table beside my bed and yes – there was the *Gideon Bible*! Thank God for it!'

THE WORK OF THE DIRECTOR

The Holy Spirit prepares the way for people to come to faith in Christ. As a TV programme finishes, many people's names are scrolled before us on the screen. We don't usually take much notice of them, even that of the director, yet without him or her the production would not have seen the light of day.

As we read through Acts, the spotlight is on the actors – the apostles and early Christians – as they reached out from Jerusalem to what was, for them, the ends of the earth. Our attention is drawn to individuals like Peter, Stephen, Philip and Paul. But if we look out for the 'credits' we will see it is always God the Holy Spirit who is behind the scenes, directing the outworking of God's plan of salvation in the lives of countless individuals.

Controlling and directing events

> 'And Saul was there, giving approval to his death.
> On that day a great persecution broke out against the church at Jerusalem, and all except the apostles were scattered throughout Judea and Samaria.'
>
> *Acts 8:1*

Stephen's death was followed by an outburst of persecution against the Christians. Today, something like 330,000 Christians throughout the world are martyred each year for their faith in Christ. We have no grounds for expecting God to protect the church from such harrowing experiences, but the Holy Spirit is always in control, making sure that when persecution comes, the church is either ready for it or Christ's grace is there to match her need.

Before the first wave of persecution hit them, the first Christians had time to grow in their understanding of the gospel and to begin to see the inevitability of an eventual break with Judaism. The Holy Spirit is often spoken of in the Old Testament as 'the hand of God' and, as God's hand, he restrained the inevitable opposition until the church could take it.

> 'Those who had been scattered preached the word wherever they went. Philip went down to a city in Samaria and proclaimed the Christ there.'
>
> *Acts 8:4–5*

The believers were scattered at the unseen direction of the Holy Spirit. For a while the salt had all been in the salt-cellar, but now it was scattered where it was needed. For a period the light had been concentrated in one place, but now it was extending its influence. Perhaps the church had become too comfortable in Jerusalem or too hesitant about reaching out, and the Holy Spirit used this persecution – inspired by the enemy of souls – to achieve his purpose.

Wherever they went these scattered Christians shared the gospel with enthusiasm. Their delight in it was all the more obvious because of what it had cost them.

The Spirit's unseen directing was also behind Philip's decision to go down to a city in Samaria to proclaim the gospel. From one point of view his decision is amazing – the Jews' total lack of contact with Samaritans was proverbial (John 4:9). But, on the other hand, it was a delightful fulfilment of our Lord's final words to his followers: 'You will receive power when the Holy Spirit comes on you; and you will be my witnesses in Jerusalem, and in all Judea *and Samaria* . . .' (Acts 1:8). Philip was taking up what Jesus had begun in his conversation with a Samaritan woman (John 4). Full of the Holy Spirit (Acts 6:3,5), Philip was open to his direction.

A different strategy than ours

> 'Now an angel of the Lord said to Philip, "Go south to the road – the desert road – that goes down from Jerusalem to Gaza." So he started out, and on his way he met an Ethiopian eunuch, an important official in charge of all the treasury of Candace, queen of the Ethiopians.'
>
> *Acts 8:26–27*

When the director of a television programme gives instructions to members of his team, they may not always understand what he's up to, and how what they are asked to do fits in with what others are doing. If they trust the director's ability, however, their wisdom is not in understanding but obeying, knowing that in the end they'll *see* what it's all about! It's the same with our response to the Holy Spirit's directing.

Things were going well in Samaria. Philip's preaching was successful and the number of disciples was increasing. This good news soon reached Jerusalem, where Peter and John were delegated to visit the new Christians and encourage them in their faith. Then, suddenly, Philip perceived that the Spirit was telling him to leave Samaria and to go into the desert! It must have seemed very odd! Perhaps he needed the angel's involvement in order to be convinced that he really should leave the place where God was blessing his work to go to what at first sight appeared an empty and barren place. But God's ways are not ours, and his thoughts are not our thoughts (Isaiah 55:8). Of course we should use the brains God has given us as we plan our evangelism but we must submit all our thinking to the Holy Spirit. We will find him placing a burden upon us for people's conversion and prompting us to pray for them. Ideas will come to mind about how best to reach out to them and, as we pray, we will find him giving us an assurance and a peace about the right approach. Sometimes he may cause us to focus on a particular individual. Behind the instruction to Philip to leave Samaria was God's saving purpose for one man – an Ethiopian – and, through him, probably many others in Ethiopia.

Perfect timing

'This man had gone to Jerusalem to worship, and on his way home was sitting in his chariot reading the book of Isaiah the prophet. The Spirit told Philip, Go to that chariot and stay near it. Then Philip ran up to the chariot and heard the man reading Isaiah the prophet.'

Acts 8:27–30

The Holy Spirit caused Philip to be in the right place at the right time. What incredible human planning it would have taken, without telephones and fax machines, to arrange such a meeting! And not just getting Philip there, but doing so at the exact moment that the person in the chariot was reading a key passage in a scroll of the Book of Isaiah! Philip must have realised immediately that he had not submitted to God's direction in vain. What is more, Philip, as we know, was a Greek-speaking Jew, and the passage the Ethiopian quoted is taken verbatim from the Septuagint, the Greek version of the Old Testament. So Philip could understand what was being read, and the Ethiopian could understand Philip.

Guiding conversations

' "Do you understand what you are reading?" Philip asked. "How can I," he said, "unless someone explains it to me?" So he invited Philip to come up and sit with him.
The eunuch was reading this passage of Scripture:
"He was led like a sheep to the slaughter,
and as a lamb before the shearer is silent,
so he did not open his mouth.
In his humiliation he was deprived of
justice.
Who can speak of his descendants?
For his life was taken from the earth."
The eunuch asked Philip, "Tell me, please, who is the prophet talking about, himself or someone else?" Then Philip began with that very passage of Scripture and told him the good news about Jesus.

As they travelled along the road, they came to some water and the eunuch said, "Look, here is water. Why shouldn't I be baptised?" And he ordered the chariot to stop. Then both Philip and the eunuch went down into the water and Philip baptised him.'

Acts 8:30–38

Philip might have responded in a number of ways to what he heard. He could have asked, 'Are you a believer in Jesus Christ?' or 'I'll tell you what that passage means, if you like.' What he actually asked was far better, 'Do you understand what you are reading?' Philip gave the Ethiopian an opportunity to talk over his uncertainties and to state his desire for knowledge. Philip felt his way sensitively, discovering where the Ethiopian was at in his spiritual understanding. The Holy Spirit delights to guide our conversations so that we ask the kind of questions which lead to our sharing Christ.

When we consider the passage the Ethiopian was reading, we can readily see the place where the Holy Spirit always wants us to bring people in their understanding of the Person and work of Jesus Christ – to his Cross and what he did for us there. 'Philip began with that very passage of Scripture and told him the good news about Jesus.' That explanation may have taken some time!

That passage would also have given Philip the chance to present clearly the cost of discipleship. He obviously also explained the importance of baptism as a confession of faith and a badge of discipleship, just as Peter had on the Day of Pentecost (Acts 2:38). Once again, Philip left it to his listener to take the initiative for the next step. 'Why shouldn't I be baptised?' he asked. Was it an accident that water was there to prompt the question? Some later manuscripts record Philip replying, 'If you believe with all your heart, you may,' with the Ethiopian responding, 'I believe that Jesus Christ is the Son of God.' Whatever is the truth about the authenticity of the addition of these words, they plainly reflect common Christian practice and the conviction that Philip would not have baptised the Ethiopian without such a confession of faith. This additional verse also suggests that Philip didn't play down the cost involved – only someone who believed 'with all their heart' would survive the rigours of discipleship. The Holy Spirit is the Spirit of truth, and those who are filled by him are faithful in telling the truth.

Stirring people to seek God

It was the Spirit who prompted the Ethiopian to seek God. Luke tells us that he had gone to Jerusalem to worship, indicating that he was either a convert to Judaism or what was known as a 'God-fearer'. If he was a Jewish convert, he would have entered fully into the Jewish faith. First, he would have been circumcised, then baptised for ritual purification. Finally, he would have offered sacrifice. If, however, he was a 'God-fearer', he had accepted the Jewish faith for himself, but without undergoing these initiation rites. Whatever the case, he had gone to Jerusalem believing that he would find the living God there.

Although we have no idea what led the Ethiopian to Judaism, it was God's Spirit who prepared his heart beforehand, by this means, for his meeting with Philip. We can expect God to lead us to people in whose hearts he has already been working. Even when we get no response or even a hostile one, what we say may be a link in God's chain to bring them to himself, just as what Stephen said was an important link in the events leading to Paul's conversion, even though Stephen didn't know it.

At first sight it seems remarkable that the Ethiopian should have had a copy of the scroll of the prophet Isaiah, and be riveted in particular by the part that contained Isaiah 53 – the most powerful and telling explanation in the whole of the Old Testament of why the Messiah died for our sins. But it isn't all that surprising when we remember that the One who inspired the Scriptures is also the Director of evangelism!

The Holy Spirit encouraged the Ethiopian to want to know what the Scripture meant, and made him ready to receive instruction. As the Ethiopian read on in the prophet he would have found in Isaiah 66 the words: 'This is the one I esteem: he who is humble and contrite in spirit, and trembles at my word' (66:2). Eager to learn, the Ethiopian invited a complete stranger to sit with him in his chariot that he might know the truth and act on it.

One sign that the Holy Spirit is working in a person's life is his or her readiness to learn from the Bible. Argumentativeness disappears, and pride is deflated. Instead of wanting to speak or argue, that person wants to listen in order to learn.

Bringing to the point of faith

It was the Holy Spirit who brought the Ethiopian to the point where he could call Jesus 'Lord' as he confessed his faith by baptism. Having listened to Philip's explanation of Isaiah 53, having understood that Jesus is the Son of God and the Messiah who died for our sins and who rose again, as foretold in those Scriptures, the Ethiopian put his faith in him. He saw in Jesus the fulfilment not only of all Jewish hopes, based upon the promises of the Old Testament, but the One whom God had prompted *him* to long for and to seek.

Philip had been part of the Spirit's plan to bring the Ethiopian to faith in Christ, but at most he had been a spiritual midwife. Now his work with the Ethiopian was done and the Spirit took him from the scene. Literally, the Greek says that the Spirit 'seized' Philip and the Ethiopian saw him no more. It might simply have been that Philip felt strongly compelled to leave quickly, or something miraculous may have happened. We cannot be sure. Plainly, the Holy Spirit was the One in charge.

HUMAN RESPONSIBILITY

The Holy Spirit's direction in these different ways did not cancel out human responsibility, either on the part of those who shared their faith or those who heard about it.

Saul and his companions were responsible for the persecution they instigated, even though the Spirit controlled and used it for his own gracious ends. Similarly, the Christians who were scattered took the initiative in gossiping the gospel. We can imagine the questions asked and the answers given:

'Where are you from?'

'We've come from Jerusalem.'

'What made you move here from such a lovely city?'

'Persecution.'

'Persecution? What for?'

'It's because of our allegiance to Jesus of Nazareth. We're sure he's the Christ and the only Saviour of the world.'

'Jesus? Who's he? How do you mean, he's "Saviour"?'

And off they would go, explaining the Faith.

Philip shows another aspect of human responsibility: obedience to the promptings of the Holy Spirit. He was obedient to Jesus' commission to go and preach the good news to everyone, including the Samaritans. He was obedient in using the gift of evangelism, which the Holy Spirit had given him. He was obedient both to the angel and to the Spirit. Clearly, although the Holy Spirit was directing events, this particular incident would not have happened without Philip's obedient co-operation.

The Ethiopian too, although prompted by the Spirit, was responsible for his actions. He went to Jerusalem of his own accord to worship the God he was seeking. He chose to buy a copy of the Scriptures, determined to give time to reading them, and questioned Philip.

THE SPIRIT'S PROMPTINGS

We cannot always see how *our* work and initiatives fit in with the Holy Spirit's in evangelism. But that doesn't really matter – our job isn't to see what goes on in the divine control room but to be sensitive and obedient to his promptings.

The Holy Spirit always goes before us to prepare the way.

He often chooses *to match the experience of the one who witnesses to the need of the person to whom the witness is given.* One of the most devastating pastoral challenges I had to deal with early in my experience as a pastor was the sudden death of a five-year-old child. She belonged to the Church's Sunday school, though the parents were not linked with the church. It happened on the last day of her first term at school. Because it was raining, instead of waiting as instructed, the child began to make her way home and was knocked down by a car and killed. Her parents were understandably devastated. In the church fellowship was another couple who had lost a young child, not in the same way but equally tragically. I put them in touch with the parents of this child. Her parents were brought to faith in Jesus, and then other members of the family were, too.

The Holy Spirit goes before us in *creating a spiritual hunger in people's lives*, so that our seemingly 'chance' meeting with them becomes strategically important.

Preaching away from home, Frank Boreham, a minister in New Zealand, had to catch a train that travelled through the night. The light was not good

enough to read by, the train was generally uncomfort-
able and he was not in a very happy mood. But then
he found himself thinking about the other man in the
compartment and saying to himself. 'There . . . is
another belated unfortunate who can neither read nor
sleep, and who, quite possibly, might like to beguile the
time with conversation.' He then began to think that
he had a spiritual duty towards the man and that God
might have 'set up' the situation anyway. His sense of
responsibility grew.

When the train stopped for lengthy shunting oper-
ations, Boreham got out and stretched his legs. Then he
got in again and sat opposite the young man. They soon
struck up a pleasant conversation, and after a while
Boreham 'expressed the hope that they were fellow-
travellers on life's great journey.' 'It's strange that you
should ask me that,' he said. 'I've been thinking a lot
about such things lately.'

As they parted suddenly, having arrived at their
station, Boreham encouraged the young man to put his
faith in Christ even as he walked home. He regretted
afterwards that he had not asked for his name and
address. Five years later while travelling on a train to
Dunedin, a young fellow handed him a Christian tract,
and to their mutual surprise, it was the same young
man who had received the Lord Jesus that night those
years before as he walked home from the train!

In ordinary everyday circumstances – such as when
we move house or when new neighbours move in next
to us – God's Spirit may have a hidden purpose. He
can order our work relationships for us to bring the
Lord Jesus to people who might not otherwise hear
about him. He can organise our travel arrangements so

that we sit next to someone to whom he wants us to witness. Sometimes we may not see what place our witness has had in the life of another person, and yet we may be sure that it was no accident that we were able to share what we did.

On a plane on my way to an Easter conference in Germany, I was sitting next to a young woman who was reading something that looked 'religious'. At a stopping-point when we took on new passengers we naturally got talking about where we were going. My travelling companion told me about the conference to which she was going, and it turned out to be one putting forward a strange mixture of ideas, basically suggesting that there is good in all religions. I shared the details of the conference to which I was going, and spoke of my faith in Christ, and how delightful a time Easter is as we celebrate afresh his resurrection. She hesitantly agreed but said that Christ was not the only way to God, and that I needed more than just faith in him.

Our discussion continued for the rest of the flight. It reached a key point when I asked, 'What would you say to someone who was dying, and without faith at all in God, if you had just five minutes with him or her?' She hesitated, and spoke vaguely about encouraging him or her to seek the light, without explaining what she meant. I replied by saying that I would urge the person to get right with God through faith in Jesus Christ who died and rose again that we might be forgiven our sins.

I suddenly felt that other people had been listening to our conversation, for things went rather quiet in the rows surrounding us! I have no idea what place that conversation had in God's plan, but I believe it did have a purpose because as I got off the plane, my fellow-passenger having gone ahead of me, two people put their hands on my shoulder. 'You must be a Christian,' one said. 'We were sitting behind you and were praying for you all the time you were talking.'

The Holy Spirit goes before us *as we go from door to door in our neighbourhood*, hoping to talk with folk about Jesus. House to house visitation is always hard work, especially when the people we visit feel they have little relationship, if any, with churches in their neighbourhood. But there are times when we have no doubt that the Holy Spirit has guided and directed us, and those right moments are enough to encourage us to keep going.

I was once visiting a block of flats with another member of the church fellowship. Generally, we were given little chance to speak of Christ until, to our surprise, we were invited in by a man as soon as we said who we were and why we had come.

His wife's first question was, 'Have you come wanting money? That's what the churches are always after!'

That didn't seem a very good start! But we were able to turn it to good use by explaining that we had definitely not come to take anything but to share with them our faith in the Lord Jesus Christ and the good news the Bible tells us about him.

'That's a change!' exclaimed the wife.

We talked about our personal experience of Christ, and eventually spoke of the importance of hearing the gospel being taught and preached.

In door-to-door visiting I seldom suggest praying with people who aren't Christians – and certainly not at a first meeting with them – but for some reason it seemed right that time to say, 'May we pray with you before we go, and ask for God's blessing on you and your home?'

'Yes,' replied the wife, 'and will you pray for those who have cancer.'

As soon as we finished praying, the wife went to the light-switches and turned off the main light so that only the wall-lights were on. As we said 'Good-night' I could see there were tears in her eyes. It turned out that she was undergoing treatment for cancer at the local hospital. Each Sunday after that she and her husband were in church. First the woman was converted, and then her husband.

The Holy Spirit graciously works *even through those evangelistic endeavours which we may feel are a bit 'hit and miss' in their tactics*. Large evangelistic campaigns and crusades have drawbacks, especially if an invitation is given to people to show publicly that they want to put their faith in Christ. There's always the danger of some not really understanding what they are being called to do. All the same, the Holy Spirit is sovereign and his desire to honour Jesus and to call people to him, remains constant even if 'the fishers of men and women' do not always use the best fishing methods!

That doesn't mean, of course, that we don't have to think carefully about our methods. We must use the best, those which we believe have integrity, and so please and honour the Lord Jesus Christ. But we must not limit what the Holy Spirit may choose to do whenever the Lord Jesus is preached and lifted up as the Saviour.

The Ethiopian's conversion underlines how important it is to God when just *one* person is converted. It doesn't matter where that person is from or of what ethnic or racial background. In going to the Samaritans, Philip fulfilled Jesus' instruction to be a witness to Samaria; but in talking with the Ethiopian he went on to be an ambassador to someone from 'the ends of the earth' (Acts 1:8). Luke uses this incident to show how the gospel was taken to Ethiopia, through the conversion of one man away from home.

I live in Edinburgh, where there are hundreds of students from practically every part of the world. There are countless opportunities here – and probably in every neighbourhood in Britain – for us to reach countries where we may never be able to go ourselves. Wherever people are from, we are to remember that our Lord Christ is the Saviour of the world, not just those of one background or race.

GUIDELINES FOR PERSONAL EVANGELISM

As we look back over Luke's account of Philip's evangelism, some points stand out that we can take as guidelines for ourselves.

Philip was prepared to speak just to one individual on his own. He didn't need to have a large audience to feel he was doing something worthwhile. He recognised the value of the individual.

• Philip was available to God. He was ready to be and go where God wanted. First he served at tables, and then he did the work of an evangelist. The tasks were of equal importance – the crucial thing was for Philip to be where God wanted him. In the same way we cannot expect God-given opportunities for witness if we live disobedient lives. On the other hand, we *can* expect that God will use our availability to him, no matter where we are.

● Philip learnt to listen and to ask the right questions. He showed tact and courtesy, so started with his companion's situation and led him back into the scriptures to explain the good news more fully. He didn't use just one stereotyped approach.

● Philip quickly got to the heart of the good news and spoke about Jesus and the significance of his death. Our task is not to talk about religion or even Christianity, but *Jesus Christ* and him crucified and risen for us.

● Philip presented the whole of the gospel to the Ethiopian, including the need for costly commitment, so that his hearer could make a fully-informed decision.

What a tragedy it would have been if Philip had not been sensitive to the Spirit! That sensitivity is something we must want and cultivate. Try to stay open to him, looking for his involvement and direction in everyday events. Don't fall into the trap of seeing any day as 'ordinary' or as holding no promise for evangelism. Openness to the Spirit is not something mysteriously achieved. We are open to him as we are ready and wanting to be filled and directed by him.

5

ONLY

ONE

WAY!

I find myself challenged by the presence of the Pakistani grocer at the end of the street. I pray for the preaching of the gospel in Asia – including India and Pakistan. Yet can I do so honestly without showing concern for the Pakistanis whom I see most days of the week in the street in which I live? The majority are probably practising Muslims. Should I try to speak to them about Jesus? If so, how? This passage answers some of these questions.

> 'At Caesarea there was a man named Cornelius, a centurion in what was known as the Italian Regiment. He and all his family were devout and God-fearing; he gave generously to those in need and prayed to God regularly.'
>
> *Acts 10:1–2*

Luke tells us, in almost so many words, that Cornelius was a fine member of the community, and that God already had a place in his life. Those who knew him well might have wondered if he *needed* the good news of Jesus Christ to be preached to him. Wasn't he already religious? Didn't his religion have a good enough influence on his life?

When Peter passed Gentiles like Cornelius in the street, like me and the grocer, he probably didn't think much, if at all, of his responsibility to share the gospel with them. Certainly he had done nothing about it, even if the thought had entered his mind. But now God took the initiative, dramatically changed Peter's way of thinking and showed the church the way forward.

TODAY'S 'GOD-FEARERS'

A centurion – roughly equivalent in rank to a company sergeant-major in today's army – was in command of 100 men. Cornelius belonged to the Italian regiment. The Romans recruited their best troops from Rome itself, and Cornelius was one of them. It probably indicates that before coming to Palestine he had little opportunity of being influenced by Judaism.

Cornelius' background as a Roman citizen was pagan. The worship of pagan gods, even of the Roman emperor himself, would have been commonplace. But clearly he had become disillusioned with those gods and the effect that their worship had on the worshippers. He had given it up. The description of him as 'God-fearing' suggests that he was probably a Gentile convert to Judaism who had not gone so far as to be circumcised.

Like the Ethiopian, Cornelius was attracted to Judaism. It's interesting to wonder how it happened. Verse 7 mentions that 'one of his soldiers . . . was a devout man.' Had Cornelius been attracted to the faith he saw in him?

Some people today find a 'religious' lifestyle attractive. Today, Cornelius would have been a respectable church-goer – he might even have sung in the choir! Or he might be the God-fearing person we recognise in the Muslim who lives across the road from us, concerned about the low moral standards that are changing society for the worse, and eager to build bridges with like-minded people of the other faith communities in the area. So what is it that makes a 'God-fearer' today?

● A God-fearer recognises that God exists and that he is the centre and controller of everything. For the God-fearing person, creation speaks clearly of thought, forethought, laws and life, behind which there must be a Thinker, an overruling Providence, a Law-Maker and a Life-Giver. The Jews affirmed that there is only one creator God, and Cornelius had got that far.

● Second, a God-fearing person recognises the value of consistent morality, and distinguishes, almost intuitively perhaps, right from wrong. Righteousness figures very highly in their moral code; they will try to live a 'good' life. Paganism led to all kinds of dehumanising and immoral practices. The one true God, whom Cornelius discovered in the Old Testament, is not only good and holy, but requires goodness and holiness in the lives of those who trust in him.

● Third, God-fearing people look for an assurance of their eternal welfare. At the least, they want to be secure in the knowledge that they are living the sort of life that will be rewarded. The first-century Roman world in which Cornelius lived had no hope for the future. It had no answer to death or to what lay beyond it.

Today's western world is not much different. Death is not a welcome subject in polite company and the advertising media desperately encourage us to live life to the full *now*, never sure how long it will last. The God-fearing person sees through this and is dissatisfied with its superficiality and escapism.

● Fourth, prayer and good works characterise many people who are not Christians. A religious Jew may put us to shame in the way he educates his children. A Muslim may put us to shame in the manner in which he keeps his times of prayer, his boldness to declare his faith and even to die for it.

Behind the religious practices of those who are not Christians there may be a genuine seeking after God. Cornelius 'prayed to God regularly' and, since we are told that God accepted his prayers, he must have genuinely sought God with repentance and faith.

We can't tell how God responds to the prayers and good works of God-fearing people today. He alone reads hearts as he hears people's prayers and sees the motives behind their good works. We are given no grounds in the account of Cornelius' conversion, however, to think that being a 'God-fearing' person is enough.

BEING RELIGIOUS IS NOT ENOUGH

'One day at about three in the afternoon he had a vision. He distinctly saw an angel of God, who came to him and said, "Cornelius!"

Cornelius stared at him in fear. "What is it, Lord?" he asked. The angel answered, "Your prayers and gifts to the poor have come up as a remembrance before God. Now send men to Joppa to bring back a man named Simon who is called Peter. He is staying with Simon the tanner, whose house is by the sea."

When the angel who spoke to him had gone, Cornelius called two of his servants and one of his soldiers who was a devout man. He told them everything that had happened and sent them to Joppa.'

Acts 10:3–8

Cornelius had been true to the light he had already received through his attachment to Judaism, but he needed more light. He needed to find the source of that light to which he had already committed himself: Jesus, 'the true light that gives light to every man' (John 1:9).

Devout, God-fearing and prayerful as Cornelius was, he still needed the good news of our Lord Jesus to be preached to him. Christianity is unique or, better expressed, Jesus Christ is unique.

Christianity is the Way (Acts 19.9,23), the truth (Hebrews 10:26; James 5:19), and the message of new life (Acts 5:20) because Jesus himself is the Way, the Truth and the Life (John 14:6). His life and death provide a final answer to the basic question, 'How can I, a sinner, find forgiveness and acceptance with God?' Whereas other religions teach what men and women must do, the good news of Jesus Christ tells us what *God* has done for us.

All who genuinely seek God as Cornelius did will find their dearest hopes and longings fulfilled when they find Jesus. Those, however, who trust in their prayers and good works for salvation, instead of in God himself, will probably find Jesus and his Cross a stumbling block.

THE NEED FOR A MESSENGER

Although Cornelius received a remarkable vision from God, God still chose to send an ordinary human being to Cornelius. There is only one Saviour, and the message about him must be made known by those who trust in him. If Cornelius was going to be able to do so, he needed someone to tell him the good news. A major problem, however, was that the messenger God wanted to send was prejudiced against the conversion of someone like Cornelius:

> 'About noon the following day as they were approaching the city, Peter went up on the roof to pray. He became hungry and wanted something to eat, and while the meal was being prepared, he fell into a trance. He saw heaven opened and something like a large sheet being let down to earth by its four corners. It contained all kinds of four-footed animals, as well as reptiles of the earth and birds of the air. Then a voice told him, "Get up, Peter. Kill and eat."
>
> "Surely not, Lord!" Peter replied. "I have never eaten anything impure or unclean."
>
> The voice spoke to him a second time, "Do not call anything impure that God has made clean."
>
> This happened three times, and immediately the sheet was taken back to heaven.
>
> While Peter was wondering about the meaning of the vision, the men sent by Cornelius found out where Simon's house was and stopped at the gate. They called out, asking if Simon who was known as Peter was staying there.

> While Peter was still thinking about the vision, the Spirit said to him, "Simon, three men are looking for you. So get up and go downstairs. Do not hesitate to go with them, for I have sent them." '
>
> *Acts 10:9–20*

Peter was full of prejudice. He was a Jew; Cornelius was a mere Gentile, outside the scope of God's covenant. 'God has no concern for Gentiles', was Peter's assumption. Jesus was the *Jews'* Messiah.

Peter ought to have known better. God's loving purposes for the Gentile world had been clear right back at the time that God called Abraham. God called him before he was circumcised and before the Jews even existed as a people. God had justified Abraham because of his faith, not because of his nationality – a sure sign that God would not limit his grace to just one group of people. Further, when he declared that in Abraham and his descendents all the nations of the earth would be blessed, God was promising salvation to Gentiles as well as Jews. The Old Testament itself gives examples of Gentiles who were included in God's covenant – Ruth, for example, a Moabite who even found a place in the royal line of David.

But there was more evidence Peter had overlooked. Jesus had said, 'I have other sheep that are not of this sheep pen. I must bring them also. They too will listen to my voice, and there shall be one flock and one shepherd' (John 10:16). Peter himself had been *there* when, early on in Jesus's ministry, he had commended a Gentile centurion: 'I tell you the truth,' he said, 'I have not found *anyone in Israel* with such great faith.' And he went on to add, 'I say to you that many will come from the east and the west, and will take their places at the feast with Abraham, Isaac and Jacob in the kingdom of heaven' (Matthew 8:10–11).

At a church I was visiting recently two gypsies came to the evening service since a large fair had just arrived. Although unable to read the hymns, they wanted to identify with Christians in the town. God has been working in a remarkable way in a number of gypsy communities, bringing whole families to a knowledge of our Lord Jesus Christ. They have shown great zeal for reaching out to others. There will be many surprises in heaven when we discover how God has worked among people we can so easily write off as difficult to reach!

And there was more. Jesus' final commands to Peter and his fellow-apostles were that they should go and preach the good news to *all* creation and make disciples of *all* nations (Mark 16:15; Matthew 28:19). It was Peter himself who, on the Day of Pentecost, quoted God's words in Joel's prophecy, 'In the last days . . . I will pour out my Spirit on *all* people' (Acts 2:17). But still Peter was so prejudiced that he simply didn't grasp what Jesus and the Old Testament were saying. It is possible to know and teach God's truth and yet not realise its full import.

Peter was prejudiced not only because of his inherited racial hang-ups but because he didn't know that God had already been working in Cornelius' life. God works in people's lives without our knowing anything about it. And why should we? Who are we to say whom God may or may not touch and show his grace to?

I did my National Service attached to a Scottish regiment in Germany. There were people I met then that I never dreamed would ever become Christians. One was an officer who had little time for spiritual things, and the other was a sergeant who out-drank most others in the sergeants' mess. Imagine my surprise when, eighteen years later, I met the officer again only to discover that he had become a Church of Scotland evangelist! And then my even greater surprise when the ex-sergeant rang me up to say he had been converted in Australia and was working as a missionary in India!

Peter was also prejudiced because he hadn't thought through God's revealed purposes. He hadn't taken proper notice of God's promise to Abraham, and Jesus' teaching about his 'other sheep'.

Another reason why Peter was prejudiced was that although he had been brought by new birth into God's family, he was *still living as a Jew* in some ways rather than as a new person in Christ. He had to be taught better, and that was the first purpose of the remarkable vision he had. Before this event, Peter recoiled from contact with Gentiles, because he thought it made him unclean. He would never have entered a Gentile house. The most awful thing imaginable would have been to sit and eat a meal with a Gentile! But that was now about to happen!

It took Peter a long while to get to that point, and thankfully God still uses reluctant and prejudiced Christians. He doesn't wait till we're perfect before he uses us; he teaches us as we go along. God may want our involvement in the lives of those we least expect. He sometimes has to do a preparatory work in our lives to get us to the right place with the right attitude.

Considering this passage may be part of that work here and now!

God wants us to recognise that everyone is important to him. In evangelism we should not see some as more important than others, whether in terms of age or status. There is no unimportant person. No one must be called 'common' or 'unclean'.

PREJUDICE

> 'Then Peter began to speak: "I now realise how true it is that God does not show favouritism but accepts men from every nation who fear him and do what is right." '
>
> *Acts 10:34–35*

It must have cost Peter a lot to make this admission. As he travelled the twenty-eight mile journey from Joppa to Caesarea, God's Spirit helped him think things through. His words could be translated literally as, 'I am now learning . . .' as God taught him something new.

Peter's statement that God accepts those 'who fear him and do what is right' must be read in the light of what the Bible teaches elsewhere. He did not mean that we can save ourselves because of the good things we do; the whole of the Bible tells us otherwise (see, for example, Ephesians 2:8–9). Good works may well be evidence, though, that God is at work in our life. Peter's discovery was that salvation is offered *equally to all*; God loves people of every race, class and nationality, and longs that all should come into full fellowship with himself through Jesus.

But though we know that, what can we actually do to help bring it about? Here are some ideas.

● Be honest with yourself for a moment. Who are the people you regard as 'unlikely' to be converted? Is there someone you have 'written off' as either beyond your ability to reach or as someone you wouldn't *want* to try to reach?

Sometimes our failure to reach people for Christ is because we really don't want to. We need to acknowledge that, being honest both with ourselves and God. Ask him to give you 'new eyes', to see people in a new way – as those God loves and for whom Jesus died. Ask him, too, to help develop in you a genuine concern for those people you would rather ignore.

● Who are the visitors or residents from other nations and races who live or work around you? What is their religious background? Take time to get to grips with what they believe and find out what you can about their culture, so that you do not offend them unnecessarily by what you say or do.

● Notice people! Pause for a moment and think of all the contacts you have with people in the course of a week. We may have been seeing them regularly, but not really seeing them as people for whom we carry some responsibility. They all have spiritual needs and it may be that the Lord is already working in their lives, causing them to search for him.

● Pray for them. It may be significant that Peter's new understanding began as he prayed. Perhaps he had been asking, 'What do you want me to do next, Lord?' Praying regularly for people increases our sensitivity to their need, and our readiness to be available if God so chooses. Ask God to give you a particular sense of concern for those people for whom he wants you to be praying.

• Speak to people! Say 'Hello' when you meet them, and deliberately try to pass the time of day with them so that you build up a genuine acquaintance with them.

• Show practical friendship whenever you can. 'Rejoice with those who rejoice, weep with those who weep.' Practical concern – sending a card, dropping round a gift, a phone call or a visit – at a birth, a death, a marriage or a special celebration, will show your concern and regard for that person.

• Be ready to share your own experience of the Lord Jesus with them as opportunities arise. Be honest in the way you answer their questions about your faith and what Jesus means to you.

• Cultivate your relationship with the Lord. It is only out of this that we can really draw people to Christ. If our own walk with him is not genuine and steady, others will see through our pretence, and be 'turned off'.

• Relax! God isn't a slave-driver, demanding that we go out and witness to six people before breakfast! All he asks is that we are prepared to share with others the good things we have discovered in knowing Jesus. Perhaps you find it hard to do this because you don't really feel you *have* received much from the Lord. In that case, be assured that God is longing for *you* to become really happy and secure in your relationship with him. He wants *you* to experience his overwhelming love for you and to know that you are precious to him simply for who you are, not what you do.

• Make your chief concern the good of the people whom you meet day by day. That will take your focus off yourself and any feelings about what you 'ought' to be saying or doing.

ONLY ONE WAY!

In the light of all the commendable things that are said about Cornelius before he heard the gospel, we find ourselves asking, 'Would Cornelius have been saved if the gospel had not been preached to him?' It's a question we cannot answer for sure, but we are given no reason to suppose that he would have been saved, especially as Peter tells how the angel's words to Cornelius were that Peter would bring a message through which he and all his household *would* be saved (Acts 11:14). The implication is that they wouldn't have been saved without hearing that message. Religion – and even the best of religion – is not enough. Jesus alone is the reality. The religions of the world are, at best, shadows of the good news about him and, in some cases, counterfeits. The first questions all religions ask are: Can I know God? What is he like? How can I find acceptance with him? Jesus Christ alone provides the answers to those questions, and by his Cross he has dealt uniquely with the problem of our sin. Every other religion teaches what men and women must *do*, Christianity alone tells *what God has done*. It tells us that redemption is not achieved by human efforts but by Jesus Christ's atoning death on the cross. Our duty, therefore, whatever our background, is to share this good news with everyone.

6

REACHING OUT
TO
FAMILIES

In my teens I travelled each day by train from South London to a school near Victoria Station in central London. I hadn't been a Christian for long and I can still remember quite vividly being challenged by the crowds of commuters who disgorged from the trains every morning and who packed in again like sardines in the evening when I returned home. I found myself asking, 'How can the great mass of people who don't know the Lord Jesus be reached with the good news?'

Since then, whenever I have read in the Gospels of the way in which Jesus looked on a crowd (Matthew 9:36), I have been afraid in case I should ever be able to look at any crowd without feeling something of his compassion.

I now know that there is no slick answer to the question I asked. But I have come, over the years, to take note of the simple truth that a crowd is made up of individuals, and individuals who begin life as members of a family. If Christians witness as they ought where God has placed them, and aim to reach whole families, then we will look out upon very few crowds which do not contain significant numbers of people who know something of God's love and concern for them.

Basic evangelistic strategy demands that we recognise the importance of reaching out to families. It also makes sense to start with families where there is already some interest in Christian faith, and particularly if someone in that family is already linked with a church. Lydia lived in Philippi, a Roman colony – like a little piece of Rome transported abroad – in the province of Macedonia. She may have become acquainted with the Jewish faith in Thyatira, her original home, since evidence exists of a Jewish colony there. But however it happened, she 'was a worshipper of God', just as Cornelius at Caesarea had been. She already had a deep spiritual interest, and the way for the gospel had been prepared in her life. It was with her, and the other women who gathered at the riverside to pray, that Paul and his companions began their work.

> 'From Troas we put out to sea and sailed straight for Samothrace, and the next day on to Neapolis. From there we travelled to Philippi, a Roman colony and the leading city of that district of Macedonia. And we stayed there several days.
>
> On the Sabbath we went outside the city gate to the river, where we expected to find a place of prayer. We sat down and began to speak to the women who had gathered there. One of those listening was a woman named Lydia, a dealer in purple cloth from the city of Thyatira, who was a worshipper of God. The Lord opened her heart to

respond to Paul's message. When she and the
members of her household were baptised, she invited
us to her home. "If you consider me a believer in
the Lord," she said, "come and stay at my house."
And she persuaded us.'   *Acts 16:11–15*

Paul's regular strategy was to share the good news of
the Lord Jesus first with Jews, together with any 'God-
fearers' who worshipped with them. On their arrival in
Philippi Paul and his colleagues soon discovered there
was no synagogue. A river close by a city was the
accepted Jewish meeting place where no synagogue
existed. 'A place of prayer' was the term used for such
locations.

It is usually best to begin evangelistic outreach
where known spiritual interest exists, with people – like
Lydia – who, while believing in God, may not yet have
arrived at faith in the Lord Jesus Christ.

INNER-CHURCH MISSIONS

I was interested to hear of a church which arranged
what it called an 'inner mission'. Their conviction was
that before they had another mission aimed at reaching
complete strangers, they should concentrate on people
with whom God had already given them links but who,
as far as they knew, were not yet committed Christians.

There are usually many people already connected
to most Christian fellowships who need to be brought
to faith in Jesus. There are the children and young
people of church families. We can tend to neglect them
because we see them around so regularly.

There are the non-Christian husbands of Christian
wives, and vice versa. There are the parents of Sunday

School children and the young people who come to other activities. Although they are not members of the church fellowship, many will feel 'attached' to it, and if asked, 'Which is your church?' will name our church fellowship as theirs. We should be building up these relationships using those links. Try drawing up a list of all the people you know to be in touch in some way or other with your church fellowship. Almost certainly you will be astonished at how large a number it is.

Contacts like these – and the families they represent – should be of special concern to us. How can we go about reaching them? Here are some ideas.

The church magazine

If your church publishes a magazine, make sure that a free copy is always delivered to them, by hand, and ideally when adult members of the family are home from work. Over a period of time a friendly relationship can be built up which may yield unexpected fruit when opportunity comes to give an invitation to a special service, or the family is in need and the church can help.

Family services

In most local churches a regular family service can provide the ideal means for reaching out to those whose links with the church are still only tenuous.

A monthly family service works best, in my experience. It is easier for people who find it strange to go to church to begin to do so on a monthly rather than a weekly basis; going once a week is a big commitment to take on. When ministering in a city-centre church, we held family services even less frequently than monthly, but for that reason we found we could make an all-out effort to get practically *all* the parents connected with us to come with their children. To have tried that every week would have been unrealistic. Each church needs to decide what is best for its own situation, and be prepared to review regularly the effectiveness of its arrangements.

'Guest' or 'invitation' services

Sunday evening 'guest services' to which we invite friends and acquaintances, as well as people connected with the church, have proved their value over the years. Again, they should be no more frequent than monthly, or perhaps quarterly.

A guest service should aim to give a clear presentation of the gospel, starting where people are and showing how it relates to them.

It is then natural to invite anyone who has been particularly interested by the message given to find out more if they would like to. Four approaches appeal most to me. The first is to say that the speaker will be going to the vestry – or some other easily 'findable' place – immediately after the service, and that if people would like to talk further with him, he would be delighted to meet them.

The second is to offer people booklets that will explain further what real faith in God is all about. *Becoming a Christian* or *Journey into Life* are suitable booklets.

The third is to say that God has probably been speaking to some people about their relationship with him and, if such people would like further help, they should simply ask the speaker for an envelope as they leave. This will have the speaker's name and address on it and, inside, a card which the enquirer may return requesting the help they want. The card reads as follows:

Confidential Reply Card

I would like someone to contact me because:

PLEASE TICK

☐ Today I have received the Lord Jesus Christ as my Lord and Saviour

☐ I want to know more about becoming a Christian

☐ I would like something to read about Christianity

Name _____

Address _____

_____

Phone _____

I am: ☐ under 18 ☐ 18–40 ☐ 40yrs plus

The fourth approach is to have a brief meeting afterwards, something I would do occasionally, but only when convinced of its appropriateness. At the end of the talk something like the following may be said: 'Some of us may be asking, "How can I become a Christian?" At the end of the service, there will be a brief after-meeting, which will last no more than fifteen minutes. If you are asking that kind of question, please stay.' Christians who have brought non-Christian friends with them will not, hopefully, find it too difficult to ask them 'Would you like to stay? And, if you like, I'll stay with you.'

Lydia was converted after hearing Paul speak about Jesus. The tense used for Lydia's listening implies that she 'kept on' listening. So we shouldn't assume that her conversion took place the first time she heard the good news! She listened, and listened again. While people may sometimes put their trust in the Lord the first time they hear the gospel, more often they will need to hear it a number of times before they understand it well enough to be able to respond.

Special groups

The mid-week meetings of a church fellowship usually cater for a wide range of age groups and interests. It is good policy for leaders to ask the question frequently, 'Can we arrange something in our regular programme which will be of particular interest and help to those who are not Christians, and to which we can invite them?' A Young Wives' Group, for example, though meeting principally for the encouragement of their own

Christian lives, can plan one meeting especially with their non-Christian friends in mind.

If a church wants to reach men – the husbands of its women members, for instance – it needs to think out its strategy very carefully. Most churches have more women than men, partly because we have not faced up to our responsibility of presenting the gospel to men. They are more difficult to reach because the majority are at home only during the evening after work, or at weekends. They are not out and about in the communities nearly as much as their wives who are regularly taking young children to and from school.

Each church needs to work out the best approach for its own situation. A church in Scotland, being situated in a rather up-market area, arranges a golf weekend each year to which it invites all the men who have any links with the church, especially fathers of Sunday School children. It is always well attended, and gives rise to genuine friendships and key moments for sharing the gospel.

Another church – in a neighbourhood at the other extreme as far as affluence is concerned – has an occasional Saturday morning men's breakfast. It begins at 8.30 am. with a cooked breakfast, then at about 9.30, the invited speaker shares some aspect of the gospel. The whole thing is very low-key. Without feeling at all threatened, men who do not otherwise attend church will regularly go to the breakfast.

Another church has occasional men's meetings, usually held at the end of the working week on a Friday evening. Invitation cards with the speaker's subject are available several weeks beforehand. Coffee is served as people gather. Then when men have arrived, everyone is invited to draw up a chair in a semi-circle. This makes for informality and means there are no empty chairs. There's no singing and no prayer – the latter takes place by the leaders beforehand. The speaker is introduced and, having spoken, there's the chance to ask questions. Often the question time proves as valuable as the talk itself. Then the speaker closes, as he feels appropriate, and coffee is available again, making it easy for people to stay longer and talk together.

Evangelistic campaigns and missions

From time to time large evangelistic campaigns are held. Experience shows that the churches which gain most from them are those which have already worked hard at establishing good relationships with non-Christians whom they are then able to invite along.

Large evangelistic campaigns have advantages and disadvantages. They often put evangelism in the news and become a useful talking-point. They certainly make it easier to invite people to come and hear the gospel. One disadvantage is that people may sometimes be called on to make a response to the message without fully understanding the gospel and the claims of Christ on their lives. Another is that we may put so much effort and energy into a major campaign that we then feel that smaller enterprises are not so important and instead of forwarding general evangelistic enterprise we put a brake on it. Our aim should be to maximise the advantages, and to take steps to minimise the disadvantages.

THE HOME AS A BASE FOR THE GOSPEL

Lydia was the head of what we might call today a 'one-parent' family. She was the head of her household, and her business placed her at the top end of the social scale, too, as a woman of considerable means. She may have been an unmarried woman with an extended family of dependent relatives and employees, or she may have been a widow.

Lydia seems to have been a sociable and generous person. So after her conversion it was natural for her to open her home to anyone who wanted to meet there for prayer, teaching and worship. Paul, Silas, Timothy and Luke – and any others with them – were invited to make her home a base for the gospel in Philippi.

We tend to be church-building oriented in our evangelism, rather than home-oriented. Our preoccupation so often is on getting people to come to meetings in the church building. But we neglect the place of the Christian home in evangelism to our peril, and we diminish our effectiveness. A Christian home possesses evangelistic potential by its influence – indirect as that influence may often be. By its family life, friendship and hospitality it can bear unspoken witness to Jesus Christ's reality in the lives of its members. So many men and women know little of real family life, and to come into a home where there is Christian love and mutual respect can open their eyes to the gospel's power and attractiveness.

Home meetings with an evangelistic purpose may be an important link which will lead people to come to church to hear more of the message of Christ.

Again each church needs to experiment to find the best strategy for evangelistic home meetings. So much will depend on the culture of the area and what may be ideal in one situation will fall flat in another. But many approaches are possible. For instance, Easter lends itself to an 'at home' meeting under the title, 'The meaning of Easter' or 'Why the Cross and the resurrection?' A Christian family can invite their friends and neighbours for supper and a brief talk and discussion on the subject. At Christmas, a family can invite round their friends for an informal carol evening, with a brief epilogue explaining the purpose of Christ's coming. In an area where there are young parents, 'Answering your children's questions about God' makes it easy for parents to ask questions which they themselves want to ask as much as their children! If a new pastor has taken up his ministry in our church, we can invite people along 'to meet and hear our new minister.'

The great benefits of evangelistic 'at homes' are that the atmosphere can be relaxed and informal, and the speaker is not isolated from the hearers.

Evangelistic 'at homes' have three clear aims:
• to enable people to identify the home as a Christian home, not in order to draw attention to ourselves, but so that neighbours and acquaintances will know where we stand, and know that we are happy to talk about our faith.
• to build bridges. As Christians we can get so tied up with church meetings that we withdraw from the company and friendship of unbelievers. We mustn't! Rather than expecting them to come to us (once we're safely in church), we must reach out to them. Bridge-

building means showing how ordinary we are, and offering friendship naturally and slowly.
• to present the gospel clearly and simply, not trying to explain everything at once, but saying faithfully what the message is.

If you have never tried holding an 'at home' before, why not give it a try? Here are some practical points to get you started:
• Make out a list of your neighbours; list the house numbers if you don't know the people. Begin to pray for them.
• Talk with your church leaders about a possible speaker and subject.
• Fix on a speaker, subject and date.
• Send out invitations. You need to aim for a group size of ten to fifteen; any bigger or smaller and discussion can be difficult. So ask those you invite to 'RSVP' so that you will know if you need to issue further invitations.
• Include in the total number of those invited some Christians who will relate naturally to the other guests.
• Include on the invitations the subject of the talk, discussion or video, so that no one is taken by surprise at the Christian nature of the talk or discussion.
• Begin with refreshments, so that people have something to do while they wait for others to arrive. Once everyone has their tea or coffee and there is a pause in the buzz of conversation, the host or hostess can introduce the speaker.
• At the end of each 'at home' tell people a little about the next one, so that they will be prepared – say, in four months' time – to receive another invite. It is best

to invite the same group of people again; they will find it easier to talk and listen if they are already familiar with the others present.

● In between your 'at homes', meet regularly with one or two others to pray for your neighbours and friends, especially for those you have invited to the 'at homes' – only blessing can result.

DIFFICULTIES!

Drawing people to Christ is never without difficulties and sometimes open hostility. The opposition may be irrational and unreasonable, or it may spring – as Paul discovered – from people feeling that their own interests are being undermined by the gospel. Behind much opposition, if not all, will be our enemy, Satan.

'Once when we were going to the place of prayer, we were met by a slave girl who had a spirit by which she predicted the future. She earned a great deal of money for her owners by fortune-telling. This girl followed Paul and the rest of us, shouting, "These men are servants of the Most High God, who are telling you the way to be saved." She kept this up for many days. Finally Paul became so troubled that he turned round and said to the spirit, "In the name of Jesus Christ I command you to come out of her!" At that moment the spirit left her. When the owners of the slave girl realised that their hope of making money was gone, they seized Paul and Silas and dragged them into the market-place to face the authorities. They brought them before the magistrates and said, "These men are Jews, and are throwing our city into an uproar by advocating customs unlawful for us Romans to accept or practise." '

Acts 16:16–21

If God permits opposition we can be sure that his sovereign purpose is to turn it to the ultimate furtherance of the gospel. While Paul made this first visit to Philippi, Christians elsewhere – such as those in Antioch – were praying for him. As Paul wrote years later to the Philippians, he knew that through other Christians' prayers and the help given by the Spirit of Jesus Christ, what happened to him would turn out for the best (Philippians 1:19).

Nowhere in recent decades has opposition to Christianity been more fierce than in China. Yet, remarkably, there are more Christians in China today than when overseas missionaries had to leave. God turned the difficulties to the advance of the gospel, and the prayers of many around the world were answered.

We should never stop trying to reach out to others because of the difficulties we run into. They may indicate that the enemy of souls knows himself to be under threat because of our evangelism.

Witnessing where we are

'The crowd joined in the attack against Paul and Silas, and the magistrates ordered them to be stripped and beaten. After they had been severely flogged, they were thrown into prison, and the jailer was commanded to guard them carefully. Upon receiving such orders, he put them in the inner cell and fastened their feet in the stocks.

About midnight Paul and Silas were praying and singing hymns to God, and the other prisoners were listening to them.'

Acts 16:22–25

The punishment inflicted upon Paul and Silas must have been painful and humiliating. It would have been understandable if Paul and Silas had thought they had had enough of evangelism. Certainly, it looked as if their evangelistic work was curtailed while they were in prison. But Paul had discovered that we serve God faithfully only as we see him in control of all our circumstances, and as we witness in them no matter how unpromising they are. For Paul and Silas, that meant accepting prison and realising that God had some purpose in letting them be there. Evangelism must begin where we are now, and for some even today that is in prison.

For others it may be a hospital ward. In my mind's eye, I can see three people who have left a lasting impression on me. They were all young, and all three died of cancer, leaving young families to be cared for by their marriage partner. But each was radiant in their faith, and their influence on family, friends, nurses and patients was immense. People came to faith because of them, including some very close to them in their families.

Paul and Silas reached out first by prayer. As they prayed, they must have asked God to use their imprisonment to advance the gospel in Philippi. They may have prayed specifically for the jailer and his family, and for all the other prisoners. The authorities might have stopped them preaching, but they couldn't stop them praying! Their prayers were a witness to the other prisoners who listened.

It's the same for us. As we pray for others God may graciously work in them. While we may not have the chance to talk with them, we can talk to God about them, and nothing we can do is more important than that. We can also reach out to people who are passing through a crisis, as we promise to pray for them. We probably don't need to say anything more than that to them, but such an expression of sympathy may be the door God uses to open their hearts.

Paul and Silas also reached out to those around them in prison by their praise of God. They probably sang one of the psalms – perhaps a psalm of deliverance like Psalm 34. That they *could* sing praises to God when their backs were bleeding was a testimony in itself to Jesus Christ's power and grace! But the words that they sang were also a witness.

If our joy in the Lord Jesus makes us want to burst into song, that and the words themselves, can be a means God uses to speak to people of their need of a Saviour. People may be watching and listening when we are least aware of it.

THE MESSAGE IN A SENTENCE

'Suddenly there was such a violent earthquake that the foundations of the prison were shaken. At once all the prison doors flew open, and everybody's chains came loose. The jailer woke up, and when he saw the prison doors open, he drew his sword and was about to kill himself because he thought the prisoners had escaped. But Paul shouted, "Don't

harm yourself! We are all here!" The jailer called
for lights, rushed in and fell trembling before Paul
and Silas. He then brought them out and asked,
"Men, what must I do to be saved?" They replied,
"Believe in the Lord Jesus, and you will be saved –
you and your household." '

Acts 16:26–31

Roman law demanded that if a prisoner escaped, his
jailer suffered the penalty the prisoner should have
experienced. The jailer obviously thought suicide was
preferable! But Paul quickly assured him there was no
need for it. To the jailer, the earthquake was a clear
vindication of the message Paul and Silas had come to
Philippi to proclaim, which is why he asked the crucial
question, 'What must I do to be saved?' Perhaps he had
also heard the demon-possessed girl's story of deliverance. Did he really understand his own question? Was
he perhaps thinking of physical deliverance rather than
spiritual? Paul and Silas knew that, either way, the
answer was the same: 'Believe in the Lord Jesus, and
you will be saved – you and your household.'

Some opportunities for sharing the Lord Jesus are
unique, and are to be seized with both hands. Clearly
and uncompromisingly Paul and Silas gave their one-
sentence answer. But it's significant that Luke records
that, 'Then they spoke the word of the Lord to him and
to all the others in his house.' They went on to explain
in detail the message they had first given him in brief.
But the initial answer served to establish the agenda for
what they had to tell him.

Notice how significant the early statement was.

First, they established Jesus' identity as *the Lord*. That is something we must never take for granted.

Second, they focused on salvation, and how Jesus is the Saviour who has made salvation possible by his death *for sinners*. Whatever prompts people's enquiry about spiritual things, we must show that our need is not just for deliverance from some immediate danger – for the jailer, an earthquake or the consequences of his prisoners escaping – but deliverance from God's judgment upon sin.

Third, they stressed the call God gives us *to put our faith in the Lord Jesus* as our Saviour. The object of saving faith is not simply the atonement but the Lord Jesus who made atonement for our sins.

We sometimes shrink from using Bible words like salvation. We're afraid they have heavy 'churchy' overtones, or we're afraid that people simply won't understand them. I have been surprised to find how often people *do* understand when the Spirit begins his work in them. Our *basic* need is for salvation, and the message we preach is one of salvation *through Jesus Christ*. The vast majority of people will understand that, almost immediately.

'And your household'

> 'Then they spoke the word of the Lord to him and to all the others in his home. At that hour of the night the jailer took them and washed their wounds; then immediately he and all his family were baptised. The jailer brought them into his house and set a meal before them, and the whole family was filled with joy, because they had come to believe in God.'
>
> *Acts 16:32–34*

Again, the emphasis is on the family. One of the striking features of this chapter's description of the first evangelistic outreach into Europe is how the church was established through the conversion of two *families*. The conversion of households was central to the advance of early Christianity – and remains so.

Lydia's family was converted through hearing the message frequently. God drew them to Christ by the gentle working of his Spirit as they listened, so that almost imperceptibly the truth dawned on them, their hearts were opened to believe in the Lord Jesus, and they took their stand among his followers. That is the usual way God works.

The other family was converted through a crisis in its life: an earthquake at midnight, that shook the foundations of the prison, opened all its doors and brought the jailer face to face with death. Somehow, God used this to convict the jailer of his sin and his need for salvation. The *message* was the same for both families, though, and each needed to have it told them and explained.

Much as it may be right to concentrate upon groups of people according to age, interests and sex, our principal objective should be to reach complete families, and especially the head of the family. When this person is converted, it is so much easier for the rest of the family to respond. Church fellowships sometimes shirk the responsibility of reaching out to husbands and fathers, concentrating instead on wives and children, and find it harder to think of a way to draw in single mothers than to draw in their children. But when Cornelius, Lydia and the Philippian jailer believed, their whole families were influenced because the family head in each case led the way.

If we take the conversion of families seriously, we will:

● pray first for the conversion of their heads, especially if those are men. Every family is influenced far more than it probably realises by the attitudes, aims and habits of the father.

● include specific families in our daily prayers.

● have the whole family in view in any evangelistic plans we make, again planning around the perceived needs and interests of the family head.

● try to make any visits coincide with the family head's non-working hours.

On the Day of Pentecost when Peter had proclaimed the good news of the Lord Jesus, he added, 'The promise is for you and your children . . .' (Acts 2:39). Paul confidently told the jailer that not only would he himself be saved as he put his faith in the Lord Jesus but his household would be too. We have no justification for neglecting this emphasis; rather we have every encouragement to believe that when God brings one member of a family to salvation, his desire is for the others to follow.

Paul and his colleagues had never been to Europe before with the gospel, but they went with the unshakeable conviction that men and women in Europe – whole families – would be won for the Lord Jesus. Expecting it to happen, their faith was rewarded.

7

STARTING WHERE PEOPLE ARE

Recently, I picked up a holiday brochure on Greece from my travel agent, and turned to the section about Athens. It was enthusiastic: 'Everyone should visit Athens at least once in their life. The city has enough sights, ancient and modern, to satisfy even the most world-weary traveller. But where do you begin? Probably with the Acropolis, Greece's most famous landmark and the great symbol of classical civilisation. It dominates the city by day, the marble pillars of the Parthenon gleaming in the sun . . .'

Paul wasn't on holiday, but he was certainly in a position to explore Athens. The Christians in Thessalonica, then in Berea, had urged him to move on from them because of the trouble brewing as a result of preaching the gospel. So Paul went on to Athens and waited for Silas and Timothy to join him there. Like any other visitor to a famous city, Paul explored it.

While Athens' famous landmarks like the Acropolis may have impressed Paul, the thing that caught his attention most was that, everywhere he looked, there was another idol! There were idols everywhere. Mostly there were statues of a head, usually that of the god Hermes – the name given to Mercury by the Greeks – placed on a quadrangular pillar about the height of a human body. The houses in Athens would have had one of these at the door, and sometimes one among the columns of their courtyards. Paul would also have stumbled across them in front of temples, near to tombs, in the gymnasia, libraries, porticos and public places, at the corners of streets, on highroads as signposts with distances etched on them, and at the gates of the city. Luke was not exaggerating in writing that the city was 'full of idols'.

APPROPRIATE REACTION

Paul was 'greatly distressed' at what he saw. His feelings were strong – the verb is that from which we get the word 'paroxysm'. He felt anger, grief and amazement at seeing the human search for God so evident, and yet so degraded by the worship of idols. Why should the city renowned for its human wisdom have surpassed others in its spiritual blindness and madness? It was evidence of the work of the 'god of this world' who blinds people's minds to the truth (2 Corinthians 4:4). Paul's anger was not directed at the Athenians but at the enemy of souls who was responsible for these perversions of the truth. It says much for Paul's sensitivity that it was the people's spiritual needs which preoccupied him as he visited Athens, rather than the city's splendour and attractions.

Our contemporary society has its own gods and

idols. They aren't as conspicuous as stone and wooden idols but that may simply be because we are so accustomed to living with them. Any objective observer from another culture, seeing our television advertisements, the programmes with the highest ratings and an average run of stories in our popular daily newspapers, would quickly conclude that we make gods of sex, money and power. The popular media seem to assume that quality of life depends on the number of sexual partners a person has, the sum total of their possessions, and their degree of influence over other people.

Further, though apparently a sophisticated and technological people (like the Athenians), very many people allow their horoscopes to dictate what they do. Many others are fascinated by mystical and occult religions or ideas, often simply pagan ideas dressed up in contemporary garb.

As Paul walked the streets of Athens, looking and listening, he saw the significance of what was happening from the point of view of people's souls. Genuine evangelistic concern demands that we do the same. Our evangelism will lack staying power and compassion if we can look at men and women and *not* feel anger at their capacity for self-degradation as they worship at the altars of sex, money, astrology and the like.

The truth is, however, that we may not 'see' things as they really are because we have become so conditioned to them that we regard them as acceptable and inevitable, part of 'the fabric of society'. If our own moral standards slip – even in terms of what we find acceptable to watch on TV – and if we allow our personal comfort to become more important than the demands of God's kingdom, then we will not feel the spiritual concern we ought to for people around us.

MAKING PEOPLE THINK

'So he reasoned in the synagogue with the Jews and the God-fearing Greeks, as well as in the market-place day by day with those who happened to be there. A group of Epicurean and Stoic philosophers began to dispute with him. Some of them asked, "What is this babbler trying to say?" Others remarked, "He seems to be advocating foreign gods." They said this because Paul was preaching the good news about Jesus and the resurrection.'

Acts 17:17–18

In any group of friends or colleagues we might get talking to today, we'd probably find the four 'types' that Paul did: religious people ('Jews'), people with high moral standards ('God-fearing Greeks'), people who are out only to enjoy life and get what they can out of it ('Epicureans'), and those who have resigned themselves to the fact that they're not going to be able to change anything in the world for the better ('Stoics'). Whoever they were, Paul wasn't afraid to get a lively conversation going!

Paul's aim was always to challenge people to think about truth and reality. He questioned, debated and argued, his chief aim being to introduce people to 'the good news about Jesus and the resurrection.'

While we are not given a full account of what Paul said in the market-place, we know that he very quickly got to the point, unashamedly declaring the essence of his message, whether or not it was immediately understood by his hearers. He set the agenda pretty clearly, and then gave whatever time was necessary to showing how it applied to his hearers.

First, he made plain that he came bearing good news; second, the good news is all about the Person of Jesus, whose name tells us that he died for our sins to bring us to God; and third, the good news is that having died Jesus rose again to secure the justification of those who believe in him, and to give them the assurance of resurrection.

We shouldn't miss the words 'reasoned' and 'preaching'. Paul's presentation was direct proclamation, backed up by careful reasoning and the answering of people's questions. He set out logical arguments from the Scriptures, with explanations and proofs (17:2–3). Nothing is more important in our reaching out to others, than to be sure that our message is Christ-centred, and that these three elements are regularly conveyed as we share the gospel. Nothing else has the power to draw people to Christ.

We should never approach people with a sense of apology for the Christian message but with a sense of authority, because the message is *God's* message to them, not ours. We are Christ's ambassadors – the gospel is not ours, but his.

We can sometimes be too wary of 'offending' people – or of simply puzzling them. And so we can beat about the bush for ages, trying to find an innocuous way in which to share the gospel with them. As often as not, we go away from such an encounter having shared precisely nothing of any worth. Paul didn't use subtle methods or clever techniques: he gave a straightforward presentation of the truth. Neither would he use 'underhand' methods to put people in a corner where they *had* to listen to what he said: 'We have renounced secret and shameful ways', he said. 'We do not use deception, nor do we distort the word of God. On the contrary, by setting forth the truth plainly we commend ourselves to every man's conscience in the sight of God' (2 Corinthians 4:2). Knowing the message to be the living and enduring word of God, he sowed its seed, confident of a harvest.

Drawing the 'Jews' and the 'God-fearers'

Paul's approach was consistent: first he talked with the Jews – those who would know straightaway the importance of what he was saying. Then he'd talk with the God-fearers, then to everyone else. On Sabbath days he took the opportunity to address those first two groups as they gathered to worship in the synagogues. Having read the Messianic scriptures to them, or referring to those prophecies they already knew, Paul declared, 'This Jesus I am proclaiming to you is the Christ' (17:2–3).

So here too, in Athens, Paul started with the Jews and God-fearing Greeks in the synagogue, reasoning from the Scriptures that Jesus is the Messiah.

Paul's strategy is a good one to follow. Here are two ways to turn it to good use as you talk with those of your friends, neighbours and colleagues who already know something of God and the Bible, or who are interested because they agree with Christianity's moral stance:

- Where people know the Bible to some extent, begin

with that and show that its whole purpose is to reveal Jesus Christ as the Saviour it promises and whom we need.

• If people are ignorant of the Bible, but know some basic facts about Jesus Christ, show them first that we only know those facts because the Bible tells us of them. From there, you can go on to explain why the Bible bothers to tell us all this – that it holds up Jesus as the only Saviour whom every person needs to come to know and trust personally.

Wherever our starting point, our goal is to bring people to the Person of Jesus Christ, to understand his saving work on the Cross, and so to trust in that work of his for their salvation.

Drawing the 'Epicureans' and 'Stoics'

Opportunities to speak in the synagogue were principally on the Sabbath, so Paul spent the rest of the week in the market-place.

It was a deliberate strategy. Paul knew that 'All the Athenians and the foreigners who lived there spent their time doing nothing but talking about and listening to the latest ideas' (17:21). The travel brochure I quoted earlier, continues, 'When you feel like a rest from sightseeing or shopping, why not adopt the eminently sensible custom of sitting for an hour – or more – watching life go by. The Greeks, with their spontaneous friendliness and insatiable appetite for talking will undoubtedly soon draw you into conversation.' Paul found exactly that, and he seized the casual opportunities, knowing that while it seemed as if some people merely 'happened to be there' God was working out his saving purpose in their lives.

It was probably the link between Jesus and the resurrection that provoked the interest and questions in the market-place. Some were scornful: 'What is this babbler trying to say?' The Greek word translated 'babbler' means literally 'seed-picker', and was used of a bird that picked up scraps in the gutter or followed the plough. 'This fellow's picked up some funny ideas', in other words. Others thought that Paul was 'advocating foreign gods'. They probably mistook 'Resurrection' for the name of a goddess. Although their comments didn't at first sight seem particularly helpful, at least Paul had got some reaction! Any comments are better than plain indifference when the gospel is proclaimed! What's more, they give us a clue as to where people are in their thinking and values.

Two groups in particular, that Paul met in the market-place, had their interest aroused: the Epicureans and the Stoics. The Epicureans thought that 'the gods' were material in essence, rather like humans, but were not interested in the lives of men and women. They saw pleasure as the most important thing in life – in terms of peace, freedom from pain, lack of anxiety, pressure, stress and fear. They didn't think there was such a thing as resurrection, and they discounted any thought of judgment or immortality.

The Stoics aimed at consistent living. They emphasised the supremacy of the mind over the emotions, and cultivated individual self-sufficiency. Grown human beings ought to be able to look after themselves, they thought. Man had 'come of age' and had no need to be restored to a friendly relationship with God, nor need he fear judgment by an angry God.

Although Epicureans and Stoics no longer exist, their philosophies of life are common today. Jane believes in God, but she thinks of him as being remote and indifferent to her needs. Faced with a decision to make about changing her job, or what to do in her spare time, she'll often say, 'Well, enjoying yourself is the main thing, isn't it?' She doesn't see any need for an 'after-life'.

Mike, on the other hand, is all for putting discipline back into life. 'You get out of life what you put into it,' is his motto. He has little patience with people who 'don't make it' in life, no matter what the reasons are. 'With a bit of self-discipline you can achieve anything,' he says.

Listening to people like Jane and Mike we may get the impression that they are totally self-sufficient, and satisfied with life as it is. And then we hear the devil's subtle insinuations: 'Your gospel is just not relevant to these people. They won't listen to you!' But to such people Paul proclaimed *without compromise* the good news of Jesus and the resurrection! How did he do it?

Capture their interest
First of all, Paul captured their interest. Paul's teaching was 'new'; they were 'strange ideas' he was bringing. Those are significant comments; we may forget how new the gospel sounds to those who have never heard or understood it before.

Although the Epicureans and the Stoics didn't understand what Paul was talking about, his direct approach prompted them to want to know more. If we water down the message, and fail to be straightforward in declaring it, we simply won't stimulate the right questions – questions which, once asked, allow us to share the gospel in its completeness.

> 'Then they took him and brought him to a meeting of the Areopagus, where they said to him, "May we know what this new teaching is that you are presenting? You are bringing some strange ideas to our ears, and we want to know what they mean." '
>
> *Acts 17:19–20*

The Areopagus was the oldest court in Athens, and although many of its powers declined as democracy grew, it continued its jurisdiction over homicide and moral questions in general, and was greatly respected. It had supreme authority in religious matters. To testify before this august body was a tremendous evangelistic opportunity, and it was all at the initiative of those whose interest had been provoked by Paul's uncompromising proclamation of the good news.

Paul's questioners made it easy for him to give an explanation of the gospel: 'May we know what this new teaching is that you are presenting?' They made the running; and this meant that they were ready to hear what he had to say. That is one of the great benefits of people asking us questions, for they are then much more willing to listen, and it means that we are dealing with matters that are either a problem to them or things they do not understand. Paul seized upon this request to explain the gospel in a way relevant to what he understood of their situation.

Start·from where they are
Paul was immediately able to show how the good news was important for *them:*

> 'Paul then stood up in the meeting of the Areopagus and said, "Men of Athens! I see that in every way you are very religious. For as I walked round and observed your objects of worship, I even found an altar with this inscription: TO AN UNKNOWN GOD. Now what you worship as something unknown I am going to proclaim to you.
>
> The God who made the world and everything in it is the Lord of heaven and earth and does not live in temples built by hands. And he is not served by human hands, as if he needed anything, because he himself gives all men life and breath and everything else. From one man he made every nation of men, that they should inhabit the whole earth; and he determined the times set for them and the exact places where they should live. God did this so that men would seek him and perhaps reach out for him and find him, though he is not far from each one of us. 'For in him we live and move and have our being.' As some of your own poets have said, 'We are his offspring.'
>
> Therefore since we are God's offspring, we should not think that the divine being is like gold or silver or stone – an image made by man's design and skill. In the past God overlooked such ignorance, but now he commands all people everywhere to repent. For he has set a day when he will judge the world with justice by the man he has appointed. He has given proof of this to all men by raising him from the dead." '   *Acts 17:22–31*

Whereas with Jews and God-fearers Paul started with

the Scriptures and the promise they gave of a Messiah, with the Athenians Paul began with their religiousness. Paul didn't denounce their idolatry, but started with the beliefs and commitments they already had.

Paul started where the Athenians were by highlighting the significance of the altar they had dedicated to the unknown god. The Greek text has neither the definite nor the indefinite article – the inscription was simply 'Unknown God'. Afraid that they might have passed over some god, who might do them harm if left out, the Athenians put up such altars just to be on the safe side. It gave Paul the launching pad for proclaiming the good news. However, he made sure he 'spoke their language'. To have quoted Messianic prophecies, or even the ten commandments, at this stage, would have been meaningless to his audience. But, significantly, without quoting the Old Testament, everything Paul said was firmly based and anchored in the Scriptures. His language was biblical without his saying so.

Second, he used familiar quotations from their own literature, which coincided with the truth of the gospel. It's a good strategy to use – people are more quickly able to accept truth in something already familiar to them. So we might quote a well-known contemporary writer, when we talk with some people. With others it will be more natural to use the words of a current pop song.

Paul went as far as he could with those with whom he argued until he reached the point where he had to say 'But', and he then homed in on the gaps in their knowledge and their distortions of the truth.

Take them on from there

Luke's summary of Paul's reasoning suggests that there were five steps in it. If people are to commit themselves to Christ, they need to understand these same five truths.

First, there is only one God; not many, as the Athenians thought; not none, as some Eastern religions teach today. What's more, the one true God stands outside creation; he is not part of it.

With interest in 'New Age' philosophies apparently on the increase today, we need to be prepared to reason with people even at this very basic level. Paul indicated in his letter to the Christians in Rome, that belief in the existence of the one, creator God should not be that difficult. 'Since the creation of the world,' he wrote, 'God's invisible qualities – his eternal power and divine nature – have been clearly seen, being understood from what has been made, so that men are without any excuse. For although they knew God, they neither glorified him as God nor gave thanks to him, but their thinking became futile and their foolish hearts were darkened' (Romans 1:20–21). His next words written to the Romans completely fitted the Athenian situation: 'Although they claimed to be wise, they became fools and exchanged the glory of the immortal God for images made to look like mortal man and birds and animals and reptiles' (Romans 1:22–23). People in our own society do just the same. Whether followers of the New Age believe God is to be found in trees, in the variety of all creatures on earth, or deep within themselves, they eventually end up worshipping something less than the real thing – the creature rather than the Creator. Even Jane, our representative Epicurean, who thinks New Age ideas are generally 'a bit loopy', believes strongly in the healing properties of a walk by the sea or through the countryside.

Paul began by taking up the glimmerings of truth his listeners already accepted, so he spoke of God's spirituality, his independence of his creatures, and his uniqueness as the source and giver of life. These truths are part of the biblical revelation, and at the same time confirmed both the Epicurean teaching that God requires nothing from humankind and cannot be served by them, and the Stoic belief that God is the source of all life.

Paul's second step was to show that everything owes its existence to God, and not to chance. As the source of all existence, God is the common father of all nations, whose history is ordered by him, to fulfil his purposes. This statement, so obvious when the fact of the one Creator is acknowledged, prepared the way for an essential background truth of the gospel – the unity of the human race as descended from Adam. Modern ecologists are right when they say that the human race shares a common destiny. What is done in one part of the globe – even by one individual – affects the rest. There comes a point when everyone needs to understand just how far-reaching this essential unity is: 'sin entered the world through one man, and death through sin, and in this way *death came to all*, because all sinned . . .' (Romans 5:12). Paul had not yet arrived at the point where he could bring in that statement, but he laid the foundation for it here.

Paul's third task was to help his listeners see that all people everywhere are under an obligation to seek for the God who made them and is close to them. God created us so that we instinctively long for him. Paul saw this clearly illustrated in the Athenians' religiousness, degraded as it was by the enemy of souls. Again, the longing for God or 'something deeper to life' that many people express today, can be picked up by us. We can help them see that they only have this desire because there *is* a God, a 'deeper reality' to fulfil that longing, just as they only get thirsty because there *is* such a thing as water that their body needs.

Up until this point, Paul managed to keep much common ground with the grains of truth found within the beliefs and philosophies of his hearers. But now he needed to part company with the rest of their beliefs, and pull the rug from under them.

So his fourth point was that since God is spiritual, and has made humankind in his own image, idolatry is not only foolish but it is an insult to God. Gently yet firmly Paul pointed to human sin.

Paul's fifth point follows: men and women should abandon their distorted, inaccurate idea of God, and repent of their failure to worship him as they should. Wilful disobedience to act on their new knowledge would not be overlooked. All of us must give an account of ourselves to God at the judgment seat of Christ. In the Lord Jesus Christ God has invaded our world. His coming, death and resurrection are facts of history. The days for men and women simply to grope after God are past – the light has come!

Notice two things in particular here. First, God actually *commands* us to repent. He doesn't give us any alternatives. Paul underlined the need for repentance by pointing to the judgment that is to wrap up this present age. Jesus himself will be the Judge, hence the importance of accepting him as Saviour and Lord now.

The second thing to notice is the way Paul came back to the supreme Christian evidence – the resurrection of Jesus. The resurrection is historical fact and is proof of Christ's appointment as Judge.

Paul's presentation of the truth was determined by his careful and sensitive assessment of where people were in their understanding. The content of the message stayed the same but he tuned it to the ears of his hearers. He didn't try to say everything at once, but what he did say laid the foundation for further truth. Later Paul was to write: 'To the weak I became weak, to win the weak. I have become all things to all men so that by all possible means I might save some. I do all this for the sake of the gospel' (1 Corinthians 9:22–23).

Paul's strategy today

The longer we have been Christians the more difficult it often is to put ourselves in the shoes of those who are hearing the gospel for the first time. But it is important that we do so, not least simply out of respect for each individual as a unique person for whom Christ died. So how can we put Paul's strategy into practice today? Here are some ideas:

• Try to remember the questions you used to have, or which you know people often ask before they become Christians. Is God there? Does God really care? Can God be known? Why does God allow suffering? Do all religions lead to God? Is the Bible reliable?

• Try to appreciate what aspects of your faith will provoke questions about the essentials of the good news; for example, your assurance that you will share in Christ's resurrection, and the difference this makes to your whole approach to death. This is something you can bring into a conversation quite naturally, as occasion arises. It will often prompt questions, and it takes the listener to the heart of what God promises us in Christ. Similarly, don't hesitate to speak honestly about the place prayer has in your life. Basic to prayer is our new relationship to God in Christ. Many people who are not Christians pray, but they pray without assurance and long to know God. Discussion on issues like abortion and euthanasia may also lead to the chance to talk about the value of human life and *why* it is so valuable.

• Try to understand the way people think, who are not Christians. From time to time, buy copies of those popular newspapers and magazines that you might not regularly read so that you can see what interests and concerns people most. As you read, think about the same issues from a Christian perspective, so that when similar subjects come up as you talk with friends at work or neighbours, you have already thought about how they relate to the good news about Jesus. We must constantly be asking ourselves, 'How can I best present God to a world which gives little or no place to him in its thinking?'

• Try to discern where people are in their spiritual understanding. Part of our love for them is our desire to be sensitive to their position. Some are well-informed about the Christian faith. Others have a smattering of knowledge. Yet others are totally ignorant of spiritual truth. They don't know what the Bible is, they're not sure that God exists, and they are unaware of their accountability to him.

With the well-informed, we can reason and argue from the Bible. If people have some spiritual understanding, though small, we should aim to help them see that the Bible has authority, and that the testimony it gives to Christ is reliable. If there is no such knowledge, we will be wise to begin with God the Creator, and his glorious self-revelation in creation, the Bible and in Jesus. People need to hear of God their Creator if they are to understand that he is God the Saviour.

Like Paul we must express the gospel in terms that are intelligible to the hearer without altering at all the message. Having said that, however, our confidence must never be in our skill of presentation or our ability to answer people's questions – both are utterly useless unless the Holy Spirit empowers us, and moves our hearers to respond. But Paul was confident – as we may be – that as we do our part, God will do his. The Spirit's is the greater part, but he calls us to work with him.

WHAT RESPONSES CAN WE EXPECT?

'When they heard about the resurrection of the dead, some of them sneered, but others said, "We want to hear you again on this subject." At that, Paul left the Council. A few men became followers of Paul and believed. Among them was Dionysius, a member of the Areopagus, also a woman named Damaris, and a number of others.'

Acts 17:32–34

Once more – as elsewhere – there were different responses, and three are recorded. Some sneered. Others expressed an interest and a readiness to hear more. All the time people are ready to listen, we should persist in sharing the gospel with them. A few believed. Two – a man and a woman – are mentioned by name: Dionysius, a member of the Areopagus, and a woman called Damaris. One was the fruit of Paul's testifying before the Areopagus, and perhaps the other of his speaking in the market-place. Other men and women – a few of each – also believed as they listened further to Paul's teaching and preaching.

A short stop-over in Athens became a time of sowing and reaping. We need to remember that 'we are God's workmanship, created in Christ Jesus to do good works, which God prepared in advance for us to do' (Ephesians 2:10). Those good works include sharing our faith, and God gives no advance notice of opportunities. We might often have to set aside our timetable for God's. Sudden changes in *our* plans, as friends drop in on us unexpectedly, journeys get delayed, or we find ourselves talking to a stranger, may all be in *God's* plan for others. Even if we cannot stay long in a place, we should still look for the opportunities God might put our way to share the good news. Then, beginning where *we* are, we must also be prepared to start where the people are whom God at any moment directs across our path.

8

TELLING
YOUR
STORY

Buying a new car was going to put quite a hole in my pocket. I'd have to be sure I made the right choice. So I read advertisements and looked up reports in consumer magazines but I ended up confused by all their competing claims! Then I had test drives in three different cars and found myself liking one model in particular. Driving it through Holyrood Park in Edinburgh, I saw an identical car parked by the side of the road, the driver and his wife sitting in it. So I stopped in front of them, walked back and explained, 'I'm having a test drive in the car in front of you, which is the same as yours. Would you recommend it?' 'Yes,' they replied without any hesitation. 'It's the best car we've had, and we'd replace it with another of the same!' More effective than any amount of sales talk, that decided me. And would you blame me?

Nine-and-a-half per cent of Christians who completed a questionnaire in the church fellowship to which

I belong, indicated that they were brought to faith in Jesus through hearing someone's testimony. I hadn't actually expected such a high percentage but perhaps I ought not to have been surprised. Testifying to the Lord's goodness, David wrote, 'He put a new song in my mouth, a hymn of praise to our God.' He went on to say, 'Many will see and fear and put their trust in the Lord' (Psalm 40:3). Many of David's psalms are songs of testimony, with variations on the theme: 'Taste and see that the Lord is good; blessed is the man who takes refuge in him' (Psalm 34:8).

David's ability to have, always, something to say about what God was doing for him, reflected his living relationship with God and the joy he knew in God's salvation. If he lost this living experience, he lost his desire to testify. Having repented of falling into sin, he cried, 'Restore to me the joy of your salvation . . . Then I will teach transgressors your ways, and sinners will turn back to you . . . O Lord, open my lips, and my mouth will declare your praise' (Psalm 51:12–13, 15).

A Christian without an up-to-date testimony to the Lord Jesus is like salt which has lost its saltiness – good for nothing. We *have* to keep our relationship with him fresh and vital. Paul's own teaching to Christians about their testimony was that to 'hold out the word of life' they must first 'shine like stars in the universe' by their blamelessness and purity (Philippians 2:15–16). Life and testimony go together. Our lips speak effectively for our Lord and his gospel only as our lives back up what we say.

Earning the right to give our testimony to others may take a long time, even years. But strategic occasions will arise when we will find ourselves questioned about our behaviour or convictions, and the opportunity will suddenly be there to give our testimony. To couch our answer in the form of a testimony may often be the best approach, in that we are not then seen to be telling others what *they* should do, but rather sharing what *God* has done for *us*.

PAUL: A CASE STUDY

Paul had been accused by the high priest Ananias, some of the elders and a lawyer named Tertullus of being 'a troublemaker, stirring up riots among the Jews all over the world.' He was described as 'a ring-leader of the Nazarene sect' and was said to have even 'tried to desecrate the temple' (Acts 24:5–6). He was brought first with these charges against him before Felix, the Roman governor, in Caesarea. Then, after two years in custody, Paul's case came before Festus, Felix's successor.

Festus soon felt out of his depth. He would have major problems on his hands from the Jews if he didn't deal severely with Paul, yet he simply couldn't see any reason for imprisoning him! To Festus' relief he thought he had found a possibility of help when Herod Agrippa II and Bernice arrived on an official visit to welcome him as the new governor (Acts 25:13). Festus was glad to be able to discuss the issues with someone like Herod, whose background was Jewish. He put in a nutshell what he thought the issue was regarding the Jews and Paul: the Jews 'had some points of dispute with him about their own religion and about a dead man named Jesus whom Paul claimed was alive' (Acts 25:19).

Agrippa expressed interest in hearing Paul for himself; and Festus promised, 'Tomorrow you will hear him.'

> 'The next day Agrippa and Bernice came with great pomp and entered the audience room with the high ranking officers and the leading men of the city. At the command of Festus, Paul was brought in . . .
>
> Then Agrippa said to Paul, "You have permission to speak for yourself."
>
> So Paul motioned with his hand and began his defence:
>
> "King Agrippa, I consider myself fortunate to stand before you today as I make my defence against all the accusations of the Jews, and especially so because you are well acquainted with all the Jewish customs and controversies. Therefore, I beg you to listen to me patiently." '
>
> *Acts 25:23, 26:1-3.*

The whole occasion must have been impressive, with Festus in his governor's scarlet robes, Agrippa and Bernice in their purple garments and crowns, and the military chiefs of the five cohorts stationed in Caesarea in their uniforms. And before them stood a small Jewish tentmaker! How did he make out? What did he tell them about?

A hope for the future

As we read Paul's testimony we see how he drew attention to his 'hope', something he always did (see, for example, Acts 23:6; 24:15; 28:20). The apostle Peter also indicates that it is the Christian's hope that is most likely to prompt questions (1 Peter 3:15).

If someone asked Paul, 'What do you mean by

hope?' he would have answered first as a Jew and then as an apostle to the Gentiles: 'My confidence is that Jesus Christ is the Messiah – the Hope of his people. All God's promises of a divine Saviour have been fulfilled by Jesus' death and resurrection. Jesus Christ is the secret of all the blessings of salvation – including physical resurrection and the glories of the life to come.' As an apostle to the Gentiles, he would have answered, 'Jesus Christ is the Hope of the ages – the One for whom all who have genuinely sought after God have been waiting. He is the Saviour, who not only delivers from sin but from death, and who promises physical resurrection and eternal life – we are assured of these things by Jesus Christ's own resurrection.'

Hope was relevant in a Jewish context because of their hope of a Messiah who would rescue them from their Roman oppressors. Agrippa appreciated that. Hope was relevant in a Gentile context because of the need all people have for an effective answer to death. Festus understood that:

> ' "The Jews all know the way I have lived ever since I was a child, from the beginning of my life in my own country, and also in Jerusalem. They have known me for a long time and can testify, if they are willing, that according to the strictest sect of our religion, I lived as a Pharisee. And now it is because of my hope in what God has promised our fathers that I am on trial today. This is the promise our twelve tribes are hoping to see fulfilled as they earnestly serve God day and night. O King, it is because of this hope that the Jews accuse me. Why should any of you consider it incredible that God raises the dead?" '
>
> *Acts 26:4–8*

A break with the past

Paul also talked about what he once was. Since Agrippa was Jewish he spoke of aspects of his case which were especially Jewish in character. He referred to his early life and adherence to the Jewish faith. From the beginning his testimony centred on the One who was raised from the dead.

Whether we, like Paul, have had a religious background, or a secular one, it often makes an appropriate starting point for talking about the faith we now have, especially if we are able to identify with our hearers' situation in some way. It is crucial, though, that we don't exaggerate in any way but simply state the truth. Often, what we share about our past background and former attitude to Christian things will register with our hearers, and make them aware that their thoughts and feelings are not unique.

When I have described to others my own experience of hearing the gospel for the first time in my teens and that it took almost a whole year to sink in — coming as I did from a non-Christian background — I have found others in similar circumstances encouraged by it, and prompted to ask questions.

An earlier attitude to Christian things

> ' "I too was convinced that I ought to do all that was possible to oppose the name of Jesus of Nazareth. And that is just what I did in Jerusalem. On the authority of the chief priests I put many of the saints in prison, and when they were put to death, I cast my vote against them. Many a time I went from one synagogue to another to have them

punished, and I tried to force them to blaspheme. In my obsession against them, I even went to foreign cities to persecute them." '

Acts 26:9–11

Paul identified himself with those who found it hard to believe because he himself had once been the same. In particular he spoke of the opposition and unbelief that had been in his heart towards the One whom he now loved and served.

Providing we can do so genuinely – and we are not exaggerating or wanting to draw attention to ourselves – we should not hesitate to share what our first reactions were to the good news of the Lord Jesus – whether of hostility, indifference or interest. My own was nothing like Paul's. But initially when the Christians I met talked about the need to become a Christian, I assumed I was a Christian, because I imagined a Christian to be simply someone who tried to do Christian things. But there came a point when I realised that I lacked something that these Christians had. Then I woke up to the fact that what I lacked was a personal relationship with Jesus Christ. I then became desperately hungry for what I saw of him in them.

By sharing our first attitude to Christian things we can then make a bridge to explain the transformation that has come to our lives.

A conversion experience

' "On one of these journeys I was going to Damascus with the authority and commission of the chief priests. About noon, O King, as I was on the road,

I saw a light from heaven, brighter than the sun, blazing around me and my companions. We all fell to the ground, and I heard a voice saying to me in Aramaic, 'Saul, Saul, why do you persecute me? It is hard for you to kick against the goads.'

Then I asked, 'Who are you, Lord?'

'I am Jesus, whom you are persecuting,' the Lord replied. 'Now get up and stand on your feet. I have appeared to you to appoint you as a servant and as a witness of what you have seen of me and what I will show you. I will rescue you from your own people and from the Gentiles. I am sending you to open their eyes and turn them from darkness to light, and from the power of Satan to God, so that they may receive forgiveness of sins and a place among those who are sanctified by faith in me.' " '

Acts 26:12–18

Paul focussed on his encounter with the risen Lord Jesus, for it was this which had transformed his life. Although our conversion experience may not have been so dramatic, it required no less a miraculous work of God's Spirit. It may in fact be an *advantage* that our conversion was not as dramatic, since that of our hearers, when it takes place, probably won't be either. We will help them most by describing what God taught us about Jesus, and what he has now become to us.

Relating his conversion experience and what the Lord Jesus taught him gave Paul the opportunity to explain what God's Son does for everyone who trusts in him. Rather than reporting Jesus' words, Paul actually quoted them. We can also introduce basic gospel truth within the context of our testimony, perhaps as Paul did by quoting the actual words of Jesus. They are words through which, in the Gospels, he spoke to us, and our quoting of them may be the means he uses to speak to our hearers.

A current Christian experience

> ' "So then, King Agrippa, I was not disobedient to the vision from heaven. First to those in Damascus, then to those in Jerusalem and in all Judea, and to the Gentiles also, I preached that they should repent and turn to God and prove their repentance by their deeds. That is why the Jews seized me in the temple courts and tried to kill me. But I have had God's help to this very day, and so I stand here and testify to small and great alike. I am saying nothing beyond what the prophets and Moses said would happen – that the Christ would suffer and, as the first to rise from the dead, would proclaim light to his own people and to the Gentiles." '
>
> *Acts 26:19–23*

Paul described his Christian experience as he obeyed the Risen Lord. Giving an account of his obedience to Christ provided scope to preach the gospel to his hearers by telling them what he said to others!

Besides outlining what had happened to him in the past, Paul testified to God's continual help – 'to this very day'. Testimony lacks freshness and spontaneity if it is not up-to-date. What I say about what the Lord has done for me in the past only rings true if it is plain that he is everything to me now.

In conclusion Paul repeated the essence of the gospel, and underlined the reliability of the Scriptures, as witnessed by their fulfilment. His testimony was

Christ-centred and Scripture-based. Whatever we say to others, it must be clear that we want their attention to be not on us, but upon Jesus Christ. At the same time we must point them to the Scriptures which are able to make them 'wise for salvation through faith in Christ Jesus' (2 Timothy 3:15), just as they have done for us.

An unseen helper

'At this point Festus interrupted Paul's defence. "You are out of your mind, Paul!" he shouted. "Your great learning is driving you insane."

"I am not insane, most excellent Festus," Paul replied. "What I am saying is true and reasonable. The king is familiar with these things, and I can speak freely to him. I am convinced that none of this has escaped his notice, because it was not done in a corner. King Agrippa, do you believe the prophets? I know you do."

Then Agrippa said to Paul, "Do you think that in such a short time you can persuade me to be a Christian?"

Paul replied, "Short time or long – I pray God that not only you but all who are listening to me today may become what I am, except for these chains." '

Acts 26:24–29

What made Festus interrupt? Was Paul's message going home? Or was Festus afraid that Agrippa and Bernice might be offended by Paul's clear testimony to the Lord Jesus Christ? One reason was certainly the power and persuasiveness of what Paul said. Paul's quick replies both to Festus and Agrippa were calculated to make them think deeply.

Paul wouldn't have taken any credit for the skilfulness of his answers. He was experiencing what Jesus promised to his disciples when they are brought before governors and king: 'On account of me,' our Lord said, 'you will stand before governors and kings as witnesses to them . . . Whenever you are arrested and brought to trial, do not worry beforehand about what to say. Just say whatever is given you at the time, for it is not you speaking, but the Holy Spirit' (Mark 13:9–11). The secret of the cutting edge of Paul's testimony was the hidden assistance of the Holy Spirit. 'I will give you words and wisdom that none of your adversaries will be able to resist or contradict,' the Lord had promised (Luke 21:15). What Paul witnessed in Stephen's Spirit-filled life as he gave his testimony to Jesus (Acts 6:10), those who listened to Paul now saw in him.

I suppose that very few of us will be brought before governors and kings as witnesses for our Saviour; all the same, we can depend on the Holy Spirit to give us courage, strength and wisdom to speak the truth about him wherever we *do* find ourselves. As we look to him, he will make us wise in the way we act towards those who are as yet unbelievers, so that we make the most of every opening for witness. The real potential of testimony is that the Holy Spirit may use it to speak to others through us. That's why we must never consider *any* opportunity insignificant.

An invitation

This is the third account in Acts of Paul's conversion. Luke realised how important an experience it was, and each account he gives has a slight change of emphasis.

Our testimony may be given in various ways, depending on the circumstance which gives rise to it, or the people with whom we have the privilege of sharing it. Sometimes the starting-point may be a situation of human failure, in which we share the victory our Lord Jesus Christ gives us. Or it may be a crisis in which we tell of the difference that faith in Jesus Christ and the ability to pray to God as Father brings.

What is important is that we should be *ourselves* and that we should speak as naturally about our faith and our Saviour as we would about anything else. Charles Reid makes a telling comment about the faith of the late Sir Malcolm Sargent: 'He was one of the few laymen in public view who could speak of God without sounding sheepish or mealy-mouthed. His faith was as old as the hills and fresh as dew. Without overdoing it, he asserted this faith, primarily for the ears of the young, at a time of flux and malaise, when doctrinal props were being knocked loose in all directions and nothing noticeable was being put in their place' (Charles Reid: *Malcolm Sargent*, p. xv).

'As old as the hills and fresh as dew' – those words describe the ideal Christian testimony. We have a testimony to give to Jesus Christ that thousands have given before us. Like them we have believed and found the claims of Jesus Christ to be true. We can share the evidence about Jesus and his saving work through which we have committed ourselves to him. We can explain that seeing is not believing, but that in fact the opposite is true – believing in Jesus leads us to the truth (John 20:29–31). Our task is not to be clever or to say what we think, but rather what God says and what in his grace he has done for sinners.

If we spoil our fellowship with God, the devil will soon make us ashamed of our testimony about our Saviour. But if we walk in close fellowship with him, the Holy Spirit will use our lives to make the teaching about God our Saviour attractive, so that we can say 'without sounding sheepish or mealy-mouthed' what David said: 'Taste and see that the Lord is good; blessed is the man who takes refuge in him' (Psalm 34:8).

9

NO THROWING IN THE TOWEL!

Some time ago I attended a thanksgiving service for the life of a friend who died in his nineties. Over many years he had been a tremendous example in his readiness to witness and for the freshness of his testimony. A young man, I would guess in his early twenties, had been asked to read the Scriptures in the service. As he got up to do so, moved to tears, he said, 'Before I read from the Bible, I must say something about this man here' – pointing to the coffin below him. 'In this man I saw the love of the Lord Jesus Christ as in no other man.' Apparently he and another young fellow had recently been brought to faith in the Lord Jesus. Each week this elderly friend had met with them both for Bible study and had nurtured them in the faith. If they couldn't both come on the same evening in any week, he would meet with them separately. When I had last visited him, he told me how he called regularly on an elderly widow who, to begin with, was hard and bitter but who now responded to prayer and Bible reading.

To the end of his life he was concerned for people, and their spiritual wellbeing.

Paul's example was similar:

> 'For two whole years Paul stayed there in his own rented house and welcomed all who came to see him. Boldly and without hindrance he preached the kingdom of God and taught about the Lord Jesus Christ.'
>
> *Acts 28:30–31*

The last picture in our mind of someone tends to be the one that sticks. The final glimpse we are given of Paul is of his sharing the gospel with everyone who came to see him! No account is given of his relationship with the Christians in Rome. Nor are we told what happened to him after these two years. Did the Jews fail to press their case? Or was Paul tried and acquitted? Or was he executed? Luke wants us to realise that these are not the crucial questions. What *was* important was that Paul was faithful in proclaiming Christ to the end!

What began in Jerusalem in the first chapters of Acts reaches a climax in chapter 28, just as the Lord Jesus foretold. Beginning in Jerusalem, and in all Judea and Samaria, his servants went, as he sent them, to 'the ends of the earth' as his witnesses (Acts 1:8). In Acts 28 we see Paul proclaiming the gospel in the chief city of the ancient world.

No ending is given to the book of Acts because the story isn't yet finished. It is still continuing now, as we follow those first disciples in their obedience to Jesus' great commission.

ACTIVE TO THE LAST

Although we are not told what happened to Paul, we are allowed to see how unceasingly diligent he was in fulfilling his responsibility to God and to men and women in preaching the kingdom of God and teaching about the Lord Jesus Christ. We might have thought that being held in custody would have restricted his scope for evangelism but the opposite was the case. Paul saw the opportunities and he seized them! Luke wants us to appreciate this fact and to draw our own lessons from it.

Seizing the opportunity

> 'When we got to Rome, Paul was allowed to live by himself, with a soldier to guard him.'
>
> *Acts 28:16*

Paul was put under house arrest. This was not an unusual procedure, and Festus' report to Rome presumably indicated that Paul hadn't done anything worthy of imprisonment. Day by day Paul was lightly chained to the wrist of the soldier on duty but he saw in his physical circumstance a God-given opportunity to bring the gospel to those who might otherwise not have heard it – the members of the palace guard. Writing to the Philippians, he explained, 'Now I want you to know, brothers, that what has happened to me has really served to advance the gospel. As a result, it has become clear throughout the whole palace guard and to everyone else that I am in chains for Christ' (Philippians 1:12–13). Had Paul prayed earlier, 'Father, please help us to reach the Roman military garrison with the good news of the Lord Jesus'? And had God answered Paul's prayers in a way he might not have anticipated?

A large number of soldiers would have taken a turn of guard duty over Paul in a period of two years. Imagine the conversations he had with them! After all, they were chained to him as much as he was chained to them! They heard him dictate his letters to the churches and listened as he explained the gospel to the numerous folk who came to see him. They watched the way he lived and the priority he gave to prayer. 'The whole palace guard' (Philippians 1:13) knew why Paul was in prison – it was for Christ. And several came to faith in Jesus (Philippians 4:22). Instead of silencing Paul, imprisonment served to advance the gospel!

Taking new initiatives

> 'Three days later he called together the leaders of the Jews. When they had assembled, Paul said to them: "My brothers, although I have done nothing against our people or against the customs of our ancestors, I was arrested in Jerusalem and handed over to the Romans. They examined me and wanted to release me, because I was not guilty of any crime deserving death. But when the Jews objected, I was compelled to appeal to Caesar – not that I had any charge to bring against my own people. For this reason I have asked to see you and talk with you. It is because of the hope of Israel that I am bound with this chain." '
> *Acts 28:17–20*

Paul was a fast mover! There is evidence of seven synagogues in Rome at this time and within three days of arriving there Paul had found out all about them, and called their leaders together. Although an apostle to the Gentiles, he never lost sight of his responsibility to his own people. No matter what commissions or responsibilities God gives us for others, we mustn't neglect the spiritual need of those nearest to us. Having preached the gospel for thirty years or more to his own people, he was not going to stop now! It is important to establish early on in our Christian lives what our evangelistic priorities are. Then by consistently working to fulfil them, we will avoid wasting opportunities.

Paul couldn't go to them, but he could invite them to visit him. So that is what he did. Carefully establishing his identity with them by calling them 'my brothers', he described the circumstances that had brought him to Rome. He probably wanted to discover first just how much they knew about the gospel, and what he said gave them a chance to tell him. He then went straight to the point – as we have found him doing elsewhere – and explained that the reason for his imprisonment was 'the hope of Israel'. The Hope of Israel was – and is – the Messiah, our Lord Jesus Christ, and the assurance of resurrection he alone gives. Although Paul did not spell it out in detail all that was behind this statement, he wanted his hearers to be in no doubt about the identity of the person about whom he wished to tell them.

> 'They replied, "We have not received any letters from Judea concerning you, and none of the brothers who has come from there has reported or said anything bad about you. But we want to hear what your

views are, for we know that people everywhere are
talking against this sect." '

Acts 28:21–22

Clearly, Paul's hearers didn't appreciate the full significance of what he said, but it was enough to whet their
appetite. Their answer showed that the information
they had received was 'anti' Christianity – they regarded
it simply as a 'sect', but Paul didn't jump in with a full-
scale explanation. He moved one step at a time, and
his first objective had been achieved: that of making
personal contact with the Jews. What's more, he had
taken their minds off the issue of whether or not the
Christians were a sect, and had directed them instead
to the basic issue, 'the hope of Israel'. This was a hope
relevant to them all.

We can often make the mistake of thinking that
we have to say *everything* about the gospel the first time
we get talking to someone about it. Clearly, we *should*
do so if that is what is asked for – and such golden
opportunities do arise. But usually we have to build a
relationship first and discover where people are in their
spiritual understanding. We, too, may need to sow the
seed in people's minds that the Lord Jesus is the One
they have been seeking without their having realised his
identity.

> 'They arranged to meet Paul on a certain day, and
> came in even larger numbers to the place where he
> was staying. From morning till evening he explained
> and declared to them the kingdom of God and tried
> to convince them about Jesus from the Law of Moses
> and from the Prophets.'
>
> *Acts 28:23*

A second meeting was arranged, giving time for the seed Paul had sown to do its work. His strategy proved right since even greater numbers came. They knew now what they were coming to hear, so Paul gave the whole day over to spelling out in the fullest possible detail God's plan of salvation. No doubt he gave his personal testimony, but his primary purpose was to tell them about the Lord Jesus Christ and the kingdom of God. He used the Scriptures with which they were already familiar – the Law of Moses and the Prophets – to demonstrate the truth of the gospel, for they all pointed to Jesus (John 5:39). His purpose was not only to prove to them that Jesus is the Christ, but to urge them to put their faith in him and find eternal life.

Being prepared for division

'Some were convinced by what he said, but others would not believe. They disagreed among themselves and began to leave after Paul had made this final statement: "The Holy Spirit spoke the truth to your forefathers when he said through Isaiah the prophet:

'Go to this people and say,
    "You will be ever hearing but never understand;
    You will be ever seeing but never perceiving."
For this people's heart has become calloused;
    they hardly hear with their ears,
    and they have closed their eyes.
Otherwise they might see with their eyes,
    hear with their ears,
    understand with their hearts
and turn and I would heal them.'

"Therefore I want you to know that God's

> salvation has been sent to the Gentiles, and they will
> listen!" '
>
> *Acts 28:24–28*

Division always occurs when the gospel is proclaimed. No one can remain neutral. A decision has to be made. Some were convinced by what Paul said. That doesn't mean they all came to believe, but that they were convinced about Jesus' identity as the Messiah. 'Others would not believe.' They refused to accept what was plain to see. They chose unbelief rather than acceptance of the truth. Those who had come to Paul's house as one group, went home divided. The Cross of Jesus Christ – a crucified Messiah – was undoubtedly the stumbling-block to them as to so many Jews elsewhere (1 Corinthians 1:23). The inevitability of that division did not mean, however, that Paul watered down the message of the Cross. He knew that 'to those whom God has called, both Jews and Greeks, Christ' is 'the power of God and the wisdom of God' (1 Corinthians 1:24). A gospel without the crucified Christ is no gospel. Paul was not surprised at what happened – and nor should we be when the same happens today.

To be forewarned is to be forearmed. Paul expected things to happen according to the Scriptures. God's words to Isaiah (Isaiah 6:9–10), quoted by Paul, guided him in his reaction to the mixed response of his Jewish hearers.

He used the Scriptures, first, to warn them. Those who refused to believe may well have claimed that they were holding to the Old Testament. Paul pointed out that their unbelief was actually prophesied in the Scriptures they professed to believe! He didn't quote the

Scriptures in a condemnatory way, but he used them as the sword of the Spirit to warn and convict.

Second, he used the Scriptures to guide him in his strategy. It is the Old Testament Scriptures that predict that the gospel would be preached first to the Jews and then to the Gentiles. Those same Scriptures teach that when the Jews rejected the message, the messengers would turn to the Gentiles.

Third, he used the Scriptures to inspire his own confidence. Aware that some would refuse to believe, Paul also had the assurance that others *would* believe – both among the Jews and, particularly, among the Gentiles.

Our expectations in evangelism should always be guided by what the Bible leads us to expect, and we can be sure that, despite difficult and unproductive times, there will certainly be encouraging results too (see Mark 4:1–20). As Jesus is lifted up, he will draw people to himself (John 12:32). In every place, we can be sure that there are some people whom he will call to belong to him (Acts 18:10).

The Scriptures teach that God wants *all* men and women to be saved, so we can be sure that the Holy Spirit will work with us to this end. As a result even of *our* witness, some will be saved! We have no means of guessing beforehand who they will be, though! Our task is to preach the message of God's salvation to all, knowing that there will be a sure and abundant harvest – not for our sakes, but for our Lord Jesus Christ who laid down his life for his sheep. There is no need to be discouraged by unbelief. Rather, we should be encouraged by the sure promises of Scripture that some *will* believe.

Keeping an open door

The Jews' rejection of the gospel opened the door to the Gentiles. It was God's signal to Paul to turn his attention to those others living in Rome. This was no small task! Within a radius of about twelve miles of Rome there were about two million people, half of them slaves.

> 'For two whole years Paul stayed there in his own rented house and welcomed all who came to see him. Boldly and without hindrance he preached the kingdom of God and taught about the Lord Jesus Christ.'
>
> *Acts 28:30–31*

'In his own rented house' is literally 'at his own expense' or 'on his own earnings'. Paul may have been permitted to carry on his tent-making so as to provide for his practical needs. Perhaps this was the only way in which he could be allowed to remain in a home rather than a prison cell and so be accessible to people.

He 'welcomed all who came to see him'. He made himself completely available to everyone who wanted to talk about God's salvation through Jesus Christ. Since they had to take the initiative in coming, he knew they wanted to hear. He seized every opportunity to preach the kingdom of God and to teach about the Lord Jesus Christ, and he did so with the boldness which the Holy Spirit gives when our aim is to be faithful to our Lord Jesus.

The welcome we give to people will very much determine how ready they are to come again and to listen to what we want to share. How welcoming are we to people when they come to see us or when they come to church? Do we see in unexpected visitors those whom God may wish us to win for him?

THE TEMPTATION TO QUIT

I find myself challenged by Paul's example. On the human level there were many reasons why he might have persuaded himself to take things easy, if not to 'throw in the towel', at this stage in his life. First, he was physically restricted. He couldn't come and go as he wished. He was limited to the confines of a rented house.

Second, he had done his fair share of evangelism! Now about sixty, and probably prematurely aged by his long missionary travels and hardships, he had served his Lord in this way for thirty years or more. He might have argued that having trained so many others, he could now leave it to them. But he didn't.

There are all kinds of temptations to throw in the towel, to withdraw from the forefront of evangelistic endeavour. It may be on account of illness or age. We may feel that we have done ourshare. While I am sure that there comes a time when we should give up *public* responsibility in Christian service, there is never a time when we should cease to be concerned for people's salvation.

We may hesitate sharing the gospel because of an age difference between ourselves and the individual with whom God brings us into contact. But why? A young person's faith can be a challenge to an older person; and an older person's mature faith can be a reassurance to a younger person who wonders, 'Does faith in Jesus Christ stand the test of time?'

We may be put off sharing our faith because we too quickly judge people by appearances, jumping to the conclusion that they won't be interested in the gospel, or anything Christian. But how do we know, unless we speak to them? Anyone whose path crosses ours – whatever his or her race, class or background – may be sent by God. That is not to say that everyone is, but we are to live each day as those who know that God is the God of unexpected opportunities.

We may be shy to share Jesus Christ with others because of our feelings of clumsiness or because we feel we've botched things up in the past. The trouble is, giving in to such feelings only makes matters worse. The less we do it, the less easy we'll find it to talk naturally about our Saviour.

I must admit, too, that it is possible to be discouraged from witnessing because of the lack of evangelistic enthusiasm on the part of other Christians. An evangelistic concern for other people's spiritual well-being is not all that common. But we may best help change the situation by the stimulus of example. We give a lead not by lecturing others, but by showing a concern for people, and sharing it naturally with fellow Christians.

What steps can we take to overcome these fears? Here are five basic ones:

- Be yourself.
- Commit each day to God.
- Let things happen as God chooses, being prepared to ditch your prearranged programme for the day if need be.

- Don't feel you have to explain every aspect of the gospel the first time you speak to someone.
- Live the Christian life! As you do so, more often than not the people for whom you pray will start to ask questions which allow you to share the Lord Jesus with them.

PAUL'S STAYING POWER

What were the secrets of Paul's staying power? How did he manage to keep his concern for others fresh and alive? There are a number of reasons we can identify and share:

- Obedience to the Lord Jesus' final commission to his disciples to go and make disciples of all nations (Matthew 28:19). The commission continues until the task is done, and the Lord Jesus returns.
- Love of the Lord Jesus Christ because of the love he has shown in dying for us. Love for our Saviour proves itself by obedience to him – the two cannot be separated. Obedience to Jesus, therefore, means sharing the good news about him.
- Delight in the gospel. No matter how great the apparent indifference and opposition, Paul knew the gospel to be spiritual dynamite – 'the power of God for the salvation of everyone who believes' (Romans 1:16). The greater the difficulties, therefore, the greater the opportunity to show Jesus Christ's power to save.
- An awareness of people's need. Without Christ they are lost – 'without hope and without God in the world' (Ephesians 2:12). Seeing people as Christ sees them, we will realise how 'harassed and helpless' they are, 'like sheep without a shepherd' (Matthew 9:36).

- A zeal fuelled by understanding God's saving purposes for men and women everywhere. God has promised his Son Jesus an inheritance among the nations (Psalm 2:8); this makes it certain that in every place there are those whom Christ *will* draw to himself as the gospel is proclaimed (Acts 18:9–11). Paul was therefore willing to endure everything for the sake of those people, that they too might 'obtain the salvation that is in Christ Jesus, with eternal glory' (2 Timothy 2:10).

- Certainty of God's sovereignty. God is in control of every circumstance in our lives. No matter what the devil might try to do to frustrate our witness, God can use even the seemingly bad things to advance the gospel. As we have seen, even being in the custody of Roman soldiers meant that Paul could tell them the gospel! Many of Paul's letters, which we delight to possess, would not have been written if he hadn't been in prison – letters such as those to the Ephesians, the Colossians, and the Philippians. Everything worked out to the advance of the gospel (Philippians 1:12). The Jews' false accusations about Paul actually enabled him to fulfil his ambition to preach the gospel in Rome itself, the capital of the Roman Empire!

- Knowing that God's word has power. Paul knew that while he was chained like a criminal, God's word was not chained (2 Timothy 2:9). As he spoke it to those who came to him, and communicated it in his letters, it had power to spread rapidly and to be effective in countless people's lives. As living seed, it was bound to produce God's intended harvest.

- The conviction that as long as God spares us, he intends our work to bear fruit. As Paul put it to the Philippians, 'If I am go on living in the body, this will

mean fruitful labour for me' (1:22). Paul's letter to the
Philippians shows that his example in custody spurred
other Christians on too. 'If Paul can keep on witnessing
even though in chains,' they thought, 'how much more
should we who have our freedom be continuing the
witness?' Paul was probably just as fruitful in prison as
out of it!

● Living close to our Lord and Saviour. This should
be our hearts' desire (Philippians 3:7–11). The deeper
our fellowship with him, the more Jesus' love and yearn-
ing for the lost will grip us as it did Paul (2 Corinthians
5:14). If his Lord could spend even his dying moments
bringing forgiveness to a thief, Paul wanted to spend as
much of his time as possible bringing that same forgiveness in Christ's name to others.

● Being constantly prepared to share the gospel. Paul
practised what he preached – he wore the gospel 'shoes'
he had urged the Ephesian Christians to wear. Have
your feet 'fitted with the readiness that comes from the
gospel of peace' he had told them (Ephesians 6:15).
Paul asked for their prayers that he might do the same:
'Pray also for me, that whenever I open my mouth,
words may be given me so that I will fearlessly make
known the mystery of the gospel, for which I am an
ambassador in chains. Pray that I may declare it fearlessly, as I should' (Ephesians 6:19–20).

As regularly as we wear shoes, so we need to put
on the gospel shoes. To be without them is to be inad-
equately dressed and to make ourselves an easy target
for the enemy of souls. To wear them is to invade his
territory and to witness afresh our Saviour's triumph as
he gathers to himself those for whom he has died.